Ready Drafted
Employment Letters

Ready Drafted Employment Letters

Mike Barraclough and John A. Nilsson

Published in association with the Institute of Directors

DIRECTOR BOOKS

Published by Director Books,
an imprint of Fitzwilliam Publishing Limited,
Simon & Schuster International Group,
Fitzwilliam House, 32 Trumpington Street,
Cambridge CB2 1QY, England

First published 1991

© Fitzwilliam Publishing Limited, 1991

British Library Cataloguing in Publication Data
Barraclough, Mike
Ready drafted employment letters.
I. Title
808.066651021
ISBN 1-870555-44-9

Designed by Geoff Green
Typeset by KEYTEC, Bridport, Dorset
Printed in Great Britain by BPCC Wheatons Ltd, Exeter

Contents

Letters and documents

Chapter 4   Employees' duties

Chapter 5   Health and safety at work

Chapter 6   Termination of employment

Chapter 7 Discrimination and harassment

Preface
The employment relationship

Human relationships are generally recognised to be complex, and in many situations can be fraught with difficulty. In the field of industrial relations, since the early days of the industrial revolution, there have been no borders or limits to the areas of difficulty that can be encountered when one person employs another to work for him or her. Until the early part of the twentieth century, the philosophy of employment was basically one of master/servant, with punitive measures available to the master in the event that a servant failed to obey orders.

A classic example of this employment relationship is the sending to prison of a worker who had failed to obey his master's orders to attend the local Kirk – he was employed in the Lanarkshire Bleach Fields in the latter part of the nineteenth century. Certainly, after the repeal of the Master and Servant Act in the 1870s the power of the master diminished, although the relationship between the employer and the worker was overwhelmingly on the side of the employer. It was not until the Contracts of Employment Act 1963 that employees were granted certain rights hitherto unknown in an employment relationship.

When one considers that in ordinary employment the worker spends at least one-third of his or her life at work, then it is certainly desirable that that part of one's life is properly controlled and protected, both equitably and reasonably. This book has been designed by the authors in such a way as to bring within the easy understanding of the ordinary employer – the businessman and businesswoman – the implications and the requirements of the employment relationship as it now is under current legislation, and to suggest the various forms of letters and documents that may have to be prepared to meet the difficulties and problems that arise in employment relationships.

CHAPTER 1

The nature of employment

1.1 The difference between self-employed and employed

It is important for the prospective and current employer to understand that there are two major forms of contract associated with employment – the contract for services (which has the effect of giving the employed person the status of 'self-employed' and leaving him or her with the obligation for his/her own taxation and national insurance contribution), and the contract of service (which creates a normal employee status with the employer liable for PAYE and national insurance). There is a world of difference between the two.

It is important to understand the differences. Dealing first with the contract for services, there are vitally important differences which will concern the tax authorities, and equally important differences as to the ending of the relationship, which contrast with the law of dismissal as it applies to a contract of service.

1.2 The contract for services

The contract for services depends upon certain important elements for it to be viewed as a legitimate 'for services' agreement and not an excuse for the employer to avoid paying national insurance contributions and operating a PAYE system on behalf of the contracted person. There are various tests that establish whether or not the contract is one of 'for services' or an employment contract. The most important is the 'control' test – this must show that the party offering the 'for services' contract is not in control of the way in which the work is to be done, nor the time at which it is to be done. The system of work utilised by the contracted person in carrying out the particular tasks specified in the contract is left to the discretion of the party employed. The person who is undertaking to perform the service must be a free agent in performing the tasks involved. There is certainly an element of equity required in that the agent or contractor must do to the best of his or her ability the tasks that are laid down. However, it is the contractor not the employer who will be responsible for the tax affairs and the payment of national insurance contributions. He or she will also be liable to the employer for any negligent workmanship or injury caused to third parties through his/her actions.

The contract will specify the payment to be made for the work being undertaken but whilst it would be acceptable to include such matters as the provision by the employer of specialised equipment, in general a true contract for services would not contain any provision that gave the employer the right to restrict the contractor in the way in which he or she carries out the work.

The emphasis of a contract for services (often referred to as a 'sub-contractor's contract') is one of business equity and a contractual promise to carry out the business duties. The emphasis in a contract of service is on defining the legal and equitable relationships between employer and employee. In the construction industry, 'labour only' sub-contracts are very usual. These are contracts for services but because of the difficulties that the Revenue have experienced, only those sub-contractors who have a certificate from the Revenue are permitted to receive payment for their work without deduction of tax. Sales agents and many sales staff are often employed on a contract for services. Letter 1 is typical of a letter creating a contract for services.

Letter 1

Letter creating a contract for services

Dear Mr Smith

I confirm the agreement that we have made under which you will undertake to maintain our factory premises at Hawley Works in a good repair and decoration.

You will inspect the property and give us a schedule of the works that you advise should be carried out at once and will quote a price for that work. On our acceptance of your quotation you will carry out the work in a good and workmanlike manner. The work will be carried out in such a manner as will avoid any disruption to our production and will not cause any interference with our employees.

You will, after that work has been done, carry out such other works of maintenance and repair as shall from time to time be required. [In these paragraphs it is necessary to explain, briefly but with enough detail that the contractor is left in no doubt, the work that is required of him or her.]

So long as this agreement shall continue, we will pay you a retainer of £12,000 per annum plus VAT for your labour, payable monthly in arrears, the first payment to be made one month after the date of this letter. The cost, at normal retail prices, of any materials that may be needed to do the work will be charged to us. Any discounts on these materials that you may obtain may be retained by you. [The payment that is to be made must be expressed very precisely. There should be no room for argument over the payments due. If, as is supposed in this draft, the contractor might get some special discounts or personal benefits, this must be covered in the letter. The normal rule would be that the contractor must account to the employer for discounts, etc. He or she may not keep any 'secret profits' made. Foresee the problem and cover it in the letter of appointment.]

There is a continuous need for maintenance and repair at the premises and accordingly you must be prepared to be present on the premises every working day in anticipation of our need for help. In the event that through sickness, holidays, or other unforeseen reasons you are unable for a period exceeding two consecutive weeks to carry out your obligations to us, you will arrange for some other suitably competent workman to be available to perform the work on your behalf. [An independent contractor has the right to decide the manner and time at which he or she will carry out the work. In most cases, such as is envisaged here, the employer will be concerned to see that the contractor is working at times convenient to the employer. Make sure that in the letter of appointment it is clear when the work is expected to be done and what provision is to be made for emergencies.]

You have assured us that the sub-contractor's certificate from the Inland Revenue which you produced to us is still valid and that you will ensure that it will remain valid so long as this agreement exists. Accordingly all payments made by us to you will be made without deduction of tax. You will be responsible for your own contributions for national insurance and will keep us indemnified against any liability for those contributions. [In the construction industry, tax must be deducted from payments to sub-contractors unless the contractor concerned has a 'sub-contractor's certificate'. This industry is an exception to the rule that a sub-contractor is responsible for his or her own tax. Do make sure to inspect the certificate and in the letter of appointment cover the fact that the certificate must be retained.]

This agreement may be ended by us on one month's notice to be given at any time one year after the date of this letter and may be ended by us forthwith in the event that you shall fail to remedy any defective workmanship within two days of its being notified to you or if you shall be unavailable to carry out work for a continuous period of three weeks without providing a reasonably competent workman to act in your place. You may end this agreement, by giving to us not less than one month's notice in writing, that notice to be left at these premises and to expire on any day in the year. [It is important that the rights to end the agreement are clearly set out.]

Please sign and return one copy of this letter to acknowledge your agreement to its terms. [There must be no doubt that the terms have been agreed by both parties. If a lawyer were to draft a full form of contract he or she would have it typed out in duplicate and both parties would sign both copies. The same effect can be achieved by the use of this paragraph.]

Yours sincerely

1.3 The contract of service

The contract of service – employment – is an entirely different agreement made between the parties – one being the master and the other the servant (to use old-fashioned, but very descriptive, terminology). The first and most important distinction that sets these two contracts apart is the degree of control that is essential to an employer in the running of the business and the liability for PAYE and national insurance contributions that rest on the employer.

It is not usual to find that letters offering employment are written to personnel on the lower levels of the operation of a business (although any lawyer would say that it would be much better if they were). Usually the terms of employment are settled in an informal conversation. If such a letter were written, Letter 2 would be appropriate. Notice that provision has been made for the employer to make deductions for shortages from the wages due. Deductions from wages are rigorously controlled by law. An employer is obliged to make certain deductions, for example PAYE, social security contributions and payments due under an attachment of wages order. Apart from this, though, the only deductions that can be made are those for which there is an express agreement which is signed by the employee.

Letter 2

Offer of employment

Dear Mr Smith

Employment as Petrol Station Manager

This letter is to confirm the offer of employment with this Company as Manager of our Petrol Filling Station at New Road, Camberly.

1. You will commence work at 08.30 on Monday next, 1 January 1990. [The date on which employment commenced is important in many respects, particularly for the purposes of claims for redundancy and other statutory rights which will be explained in later chapters.]

2. You are employed as Manager of the Filling Station at Main Road, Newtown and will undertake such duties as may from time to time be delegated to you as part of that employment. [The job should be described by a general job description. The actual details of duties to be performed can be dealt with by general instructions given in the course of the employment.]

3. You will be paid at the rate of £250 per week with overtime rates of £5 per hour. Wages are reviewed annually on 1 December every year and take effect from 1 January following the review. [The wages must be set out including any overtime rates.]

4. You will be paid fortnightly in arrears, the first payment being made on 12 January and on every second Friday thereafter. Payment will be made by cheque. [Pay days must be fixed.]

5. Your hours of work are from 08.30 to 17.00 Monday to Friday and you may be required to work additional hours on those days or, with your agreement, on Saturdays and Sundays. [If it is expected that the employer will have the right to call for overtime working, this must be included in the letter of appointment.]

6. (a) You will be entitled to three weeks' holiday in every year, not more than two of which can be taken consecutively. The holiday year commences on 1 January in each year. Holidays not taken in any year cannot be carried foward to the next year. Holidays must be agreed in advance with me. In the event that your employment is terminated you will be entitled to be paid holiday pay for any holiday days not taken. The pay will be calculated at the rate equal to your normal weekly wage excluding overtime. You will receive one-seventh of this wage for each day's holiday you have not taken. Your entitlement to holiday is in addition to public holidays. [There is no general right to holiday pay. The rights to holidays and payment of holiday pay for holidays not taken must be part of the agreement and should be set out.]

    (b) If you are unable to work because of sickness or injury, you will be entitled to be paid at your normal rate of pay for the first four weeks of illness or injury. There will be deducted from your pay the amount of state sickness benefit you are entitled to receive. After four weeks the position will be reviewed and any continuance of pay will be at the discretion of the employer. [Chapter 3 will explain the right to sick pay. The position should be dealt with on appointment, if only to let the employee know what is proposed.]

    (c) There is no Company Pension Scheme under which you will be entitled to benefit and there is no contracting out certificate in force under the Social Security Pensions Act 1975. [Whether 'contracted in' or 'contracted out' for pension must be explained.]

7. You are entitled to receive four weeks' notice to determine your employment and you are obliged to give four weeks' notice o

your intention to leave. [Four weeks is the usual period. It can be more – for a senior employee it probably would be more – it can be as little as one week. Again, this will be explained later, in Chapter 6.]

8. The Company has not adopted any formal disciplinary code. You will obey the instructions as to your work which you are given by the Area Manager. If you are dissatisfied with any disciplinary decision which relates to you, you should first refer the matter to me at this address. If you are not satisfied with my decision you may appeal directly to the General Manager. To do this you should inform his Secretary and request a meeting with the General Manager. In case of urgency or where the General Manager is for any reason not available you should appeal directly to the Company Secretary at head office. [The employee has to be told of any disciplinary code that affects him or her.]

9. You will be solely responsible for the cash collected at this Station. At the end of each day, you will cash up, reconcile the takings with the petrol, oil and other goods sold. You will make a return to the accounts department here of cash taken and sales made each day. This return will be made on the forms which will be supplied to you. You will pay the cash taken into the night safe deposit box of the bank. In the event that the cash collected is less than the value of the sales made, the deficiency, to the full extent permitted by law, will be deducted from the wages due to you at the next payday.

I do hope that you will be joining us and to record your acceptance of these terms, and in particular your agreement to the right to deduct cash shortages from your wages, I would be grateful if you could sign and return to me in the enclosed stamped and addressed envelope one copy of this letter. [There are very limited rights for an employer to make deductions from wages. Where any such rights are wanted the employee must give his or her agreement in writing.]

Yours sincerely

Personnel Manager

It may be that an appointment is to be made on a probation- ary basis. In this event the paragraph which is suggested in Chapter 4 (Letter 27) should be added.

There are occasions when an employee has to be engaged to replace some other employee who is absent through sickness or through pregnancy. The replacement, if nothing is said, could become entitled to protection from dismissal, if he or she is employed for more than two years (not an impossible situation in the case of a long-term illness). The employer can protect him- or herself against that possibility by giving notice at the time of the engagement of the replacement that the employment is likely to end. Letter 3 could be written to give this notice.

Letter 3

Letter notifying possibility of dismissal on return of a sick employee

Dear

This is to confirm to you that your employment as chef in our works canteen has been made because of the need of our regular chef to undergo medical treatment. We do not know how long his treatment may last. When he is fit to resume his normal duties, we must warn you that it is probable that your employment may be terminated.

Yours sincerely

Personnel Manager

1.4 Statement of terms and conditions of employment

The fact that there is nothing in writing does not mean that there is no contract. On the contrary, there has always been a 'contractual' relationship in the employment of labour. Prior to the Contracts of Employment Act 1963, however, the relation- ship was usually defined as an implied contractual agreement, with the emphasis on 'implied'. Even after twenty-six years of on-going legislation concerned with the regularisation of the employment relationship, there are many employers who fail either to issue a statement of particulars or, indeed, have any written form of contract whatsoever. It is the law that a statement of the terms of employment must be given to an employee. The Contracts of Employment Act 1963 laid down for the first time the right of an employee – employed within the United Kingdom – to be given a statement of the terms and conditions of the employment he or she was entering into. The employer was now required to issue this statement within a certain limited period after the employee had been hired. The development of a legal structure designed to offer the employee a degree of employment protection thus developed over the next twenty years, with various other Acts and Regulations being enacted and passed by the various governments, which ensured that the employer/employee relationship was better organised and regularised. Document 1 is a typical form of statement of particulars. This document is not the contract but it does help to show what the contract terms are. Each of the headings 1–10 have to be covered. The information can be set out in a written contract.

If Letter 2 is written, a statement in the form of Document 1 should still be given because the letter is only an offer of employment and when it has been accepted (in all probability by a telephone call, or even perhaps by just turning up for work) its terms need to be recorded in the formal manner required by the statute. The statement need not be too precise in spelling out every item. It can, for example, short circuit a lengthy exposition by making reference to matters to be contained in another document (such as a staff handbook) to which attention is drawn and of which a copy is available to the employee.

Document 1

Statement of terms and conditions of employment

This notice is given to you pursuant to the provisions of the Employment Protection Act 1975 as amended.

1. Your employer is John Smith (1985) Limited. [It is often the case that, in a group of companies, staff are employed by a company whilst the outside world knows the same business under a totally different name. The employee must be told the name of the company by whom he or she is employed and against whom he or she has rights.]

2. Your employment commenced on 1 January 1990. [The date on which employment commences becomes very important when certain rights are considered. This will be explained later, p. 13.]

3. There is no employment with a previous employer which counts as part of your continuous employment. [It is possible, for example where a business has been taken over or where an employee has been transferred from one job to another, that the employee has previously been employed by another company in the group or in a business acquired by the group. In this case it is probable that he or she has the right in law to be regarded as having been continuously employed by the same employer, even though in law that is not so. The employee must be told whether or not this is the case. Notice the section on redundancy – Chapter 6, Section 6.]

4. You will be paid at the rate of   per hour with overtime rates of   . [The employee must be told how his or her pay is to be calculated and will have to be given details with each pay packet to enable him/her to check that the amount received is correct.]

5. You will be paid fortnightly in arrears, the first payment being made on 12 January and on every second Friday thereafter. [The employee has to be told the intervals between each pay day and when the payday is to be.]

6. Your hours of work are from 08.30 to 17.00 Monday to Friday and you may be required to work additional hours on those days, or, with your agreement, on Saturdays and Sundays. [The employee must be told the normal working hours.]

7. (a) You will be entitled to three weeks' holiday in every year, not more than two of which can be taken consecutively. The holiday year commences on 1 January in each year. Holidays not taken in any year cannot be carried forward to the next year. Holidays must be agreed in advance with the Works Supervisor. In the event that your employment is terminated you will be entitled to be paid holiday pay for

any holiday days not taken. The pay will be calculated at the rate equal to your normal weekly wage excluding overtime. You will receive one-seventh of this wage for each day's holiday you have not taken. Your entitlement to holiday is in addition to public holidays. [The employee must be told of his or her holiday rights and in the case of holiday pay must be told how this is calculated so as to enable him/her to calculate it precisely.]

(b) If you are unable to work because of sickness or injury, you will be entitled to be paid at your normal rate of pay for the first four weeks of illness or injury. There will be deducted from your pay the amount of state sickness benefit you are entitled to receive. After four weeks the position will be reviewed and any continuance of pay will be at the discretion of the employer. [Again, the employee's rights must be clearly explained and his/her rights to sick pay set out so that he/she can see that a just entitlement is being received.]

(c) There is no Company Pension Scheme under which you will be entitled to benefit and there is no contracting out certificate in force under the Social Security Pensions Act 1975. [The employee must know whether the company is contracted in or out of the state scheme so that he or she can make proper arrangements.]

8. You are entitled to receive four weeks' notice to terminate your employment and you are obliged to give four weeks' notice of your intention to leave. [The employee must be told the contractual position as it relates to him or her. The legal provisions that are discussed later are imposed by statute and need not be explained. Four weeks, as chosen here, is probably an unusually long period in a weekly employment but it is chosen to illustrate the point that there is not a 'normal' period of notice.]

9. You are employed as warehouseman at the warehouse in Burgh Enterprise Park. [The employee has to be told what the job is.]

10. The Company's code of discipline is set out in the works handbook, a copy of, which is available for you in the Supervisor's office. You will obey the instructions as to your work which are given by the Works Supervisor. If you are dissatisfied with any disciplinary decision which relates to you, you should

first refer the matter to the Works Supervisor. If you are not satisfied with his decision you may appeal directly to the Works Manager. To do this you should inform the Manager's Secretary in his office and request a meeting with the Manager. In case of urgency or where the Manager is for any reason not available you should appeal directly to the Company Secretary at Head Office. [The code of discipline, if it exists, must be available and the employee must know where it is and be able to find out what it says. He or she must also be told clearly of his/her rights to challenge disciplinary decisions and any rights of appeal. In particular, he/she must know the individual to whom he/she can refer.]

1.5 Formal contract of employment

For more senior employees it would be usual to provide a formal contract of employment. Document 2 is such a contract. The principles underlying a formal contractual document and those applying to a contract made by letter are exactly the same. A formal contract is usually chosen for a senior employee because it is expected to have a longer-term effect and will need to cover in detail those questions, which are discussed in Chapter 4, of confidentiality, restriction on competition and duty of loyalty.

Document 2

Formal contract of employment

THIS AGREEMENT is made the   day of   1990

BETWEEN: Chelmsford Industrial Workshops Limited of The Essex Trading Estate, Chelmsford, Essex (the Company)   1. and William Arthur Brown of 64 Wickford Street, Chelmsford, Essex (the Executive)   2.

WHEREBY IT IS AGREED as follows

1. The Company will employ the Executive and the Executive will serve the Company as its Production Director upon the terms

of this Agreement. [In this clause it is necessary to set out the brief job title but not the detailed job description.]

2. This appointment shall commence on the date hereof and (subject as hereinafter provided) shall continue thereafter unless and until determined by either party giving to the other not less than three months' notice in writing expiring on or at any time after the third anniversary of the date hereof. [In this clause the starting date must be named. If for some reason the employment had started before the date of the agreement it would be necessary to say the day on which it started and that from that date to the date of the agreement the employment had been 'on the terms herein contained'. The clause should also say how long the employment is intended to last. It may be for a set period; it may be until ended by written notice; or it may be, as suggested here, for a set period and then until determined by notice.]

3. (a) The Executive shall well and faithfully serve the Company and the Group and use his best endeavours to promote, develop and extend the interests and business of the Company and the Group. [Some expressions will have to be defined, such as 'the Group'. Rather than dot definitions throughout the documents so that it is difficult to find them, add a special definitions clause or appendix.]

   (b) The Executive shall perform such duties and exercise such powers in relation to the conduct and management of the Company and the Group as may from time to time be assigned to or vested in him by the Board and shall at all times and in all respects conform to and comply with all directions and regulations made by the Board as are communicated to him by the Directors. [Clause 1 gave a job title. For a senior executive, rather than give a detailed job specification it would be usual to use a provision such as this which enables the executive to use his or her talents in the most effective way by giving him/her tasks to perform over the whole range of activities that could be expected to come within the job title.]

   (c) The Executive shall unless prevented by ill health from so doing devote the whole of his time and attention to the business affairs of the Company and the Group.

   (d) The Executive shall not directly or indirectly enter into or be concerned or interested in any other business or occupation whatsoever except with the consent in writing of the Board, which consent may be given subject to any terms and conditions which the Board may reasonably impose and any breach of such terms and conditions shall be deemed to be a breach of the terms of this Agreement. [It is necessary to use these clauses if it is intended to prevent the Executive having any business interest outside the Company. Sub-clause (c) is the 'whole time and attention' clause which implies by law what sub-clause (d) expressly sets out. Without these clauses he or she is free to 'moonlight' and develop his/her own business interests outside working hours.]

(e) Nothing in this Agreement shall be deemed to preclude the Executive from holding or being otherwise interested in any shares or other securities of any Company where such shares or securities are held by way of investment only and are shares or securities of a Company whose shares are for the time being listed or dealt with (regularly or from time to time) in accordance with the rules of any recognised stock exchange and the interest of the Executive therein does not extend to more than 3 per cent of the aggregate amount of the securities. [Obviously, the Executive must be allowed normal investment opportunities and this clause protects him or her against the suggestion that his/her investments are a technical breach of the Agreement. It is usual to limit the investment to normal stock exchange investments since investment in a private company raises the question whether that is not the first step on the way to him/her becoming more deeply involved.]

(f) For the purposes of this clause 'occupation' shall include membership of parliament or any other public or private work or office which in the opinion of the Board may hinder or otherwise interfere with the performance by the Executive of his duties under this Agreement. [Political activity would not normally be within the type of restriction that sub-clauses (c) and (d) are aimed at. Political activity can, though, become a problem, particularly if there are aspirations for political office. This clause allows the Company to keep some control over the situation. Trade union activity is more difficult. Chapter 4 will discuss the rights to engage in union affairs.]

4. The Company shall pay to the Executive by way of remuneration for his services hereunder:

    (a) At a salary at the rate of £25,000 per annum which will accrue from day to day and will be payable by equal instalments in arrears on the last working day in each calendar month and will be inclusive of any fees receivable by the Executive as a Director of any member of the Group. [The salary has to be stated. In the case of a senior executive it is very probable that he or she may be appointed a Director of one or more of the subsidiary companies. It must be made clear, that that appointment carries no extra right to Directors' fees and that his/her salary is inclusive of all Directors' fees.]

    (b) Such increment to that salary as shall be determined by review at the absolute discretion of the Board having given due consideration to the performance of the Executive since the last review date with effect from 1 June in each year of service (the 'review date') or on the first business day after the review date in the event of that date falling on a non-business day. The first review date shall be 1 June 1991. [Some provision should be made for increases. An automatic increase related to some index could be chosen. It must be remembered by the Company that an automatic increase will entitle the Executive to that increase even if he or she has not merited it or if the Company's finances cannot justify it. It must be remembered by the Executive that an automatic increase means that no matter how much he or she may deserve a higher increase, the automatic increase has a set limit.]

5. In addition to his remuneration hereunder, the Executive shall (on production of such receipts and vouchers as the Company may require) be reimbursed by the Company for all reasonable expenses properly incurred by him in the discharge of his duties hereunder. [It would be usual to lay down a Company policy on such matter as whether or not first class travel is expected, the standard of hotels and restaurants to be used

and matters of that nature. These should be left to be imposed by internal regulation, rather than be spelled out in a service agreement.]

6. (a) The Company shall during the Executive's employment hereunder and whilst the Executive is legally entitled to drive a motor car, provide the Executive with a motor car commensurate with his status in the Company (the decision as to the suitability of such car being in case of dispute at the absolute discretion of the Board), such car being provided to the Executive for use in performance of his duties hereunder. The Company shall as hereinafter provided pay all taxation, insurance premiums and the running expenses in respect of such motor car including petrol, oil, maintenance and repairs.

   (b) The Executive shall be permitted reasonable use of the motor car for his own private purposes.

   (c) The Executive shall at all times conform with all regulations which may from time to time be imposed by the Company in regard to motor cars provided by the Company for use by its officers and employees. [The motor car takes an ever increasing importance in the employment package demanded by senior employees. For this reason the agreement should deal with the question in rather more detail than is really justified. To cover all possibilities, sub-clause (c) is included.]

7. The Executive shall be entitled in addition to the statutory holidays to twenty-one working days' holiday in each calendar year to be taken at such time or times as may be approved by the Board provided that a maximum of two weeks in any one year maybe taken together and no holiday entitlement may be accrued or carried forward from year to year.

8. Without prejudice to every other duty of confidentiality imposed upon him to keep secret all information given or gained by him in confidence the Executive will [as is discussed in a later chapter, there is a duty of confidence which the law imposes upon all employees. This clause is attempting to explain and extend that duty]:

   (a) neither during or after the end of his employment by the Company without due authorisation by the Company or as a necessary part of the performance of his duties hereunder disclose to any person or make use of such confidential information.

(b) deliver up to the Company immediately at the end of his employment all documents and property belonging to the Company which are in his possession including documents made by him in the course of his employment.

(c) not at any time make any copy, abstract summary or précis of the whole or any part of a document belonging to the Company except when required to do so in the course of his employment in which event such copy, summary or précis shall belong to the Company.

9. The Executive's employment hereunder may be terminated by the Company forthwith if:

(a) the Executive shall become bankrupt or make any arrangement or composition with his creditors generally. [Problems arise from the employment of a bankrupt. Firstly, he or she is prohibited from being a director or a manager of a business. Secondly, the bankrupt's earnings, in so far as they exceed what is reasonably necessary, can be taken by his/her trustee in bankruptcy. Thirdly, of course, there is the effect on those dealing with the bankrupt who know of his/her misfortune and may draw adverse conclusions.]

(b) the Executive shall be disqualified from being a Director of a Company. [Quite apart from insolvency, there are various Acts of Parliament which enable either the Court or the Secretary of State to make a disqualification order.]

(c) the Executive shall be guilty of serious misconduct in connection with the duties delegated to him by the Board or affecting the business of the Company or if without reasonable cause the Executive neglects or fails to discharge such duties or regulations as are referred to in clause 3(b) hereof or he fails to observe and perform in all material respects the terms and provisions of this Agreement.

(d) the Executive shall be convicted of an offence which is capable of being tried on indictment. [This excludes the minor traffic offence, which can only be tried summarily (i.e. before a magistrate). Some offences are triable on indictment only, that means on a formal charge that will have to be tried in a Crown Court – they are the more serious offences. Some offences which involve dishonesty, petty theft for example, can be tried summarily or tried on indictment.]

(e) the Executive shall be unable to fulfil his duties hereunder through illness, accident or mental or physical incapacity for a continuous period of twenty-six weeks or any periods totalling twenty-six weeks in any period of fifty-two weeks. [This is possibly the most difficult situation, where an otherwise valued employee falls ill and cannot work for a long time. Some power has to be retained to use that incapacity as a ground to determine the contract.]

10. For the purposes of determining whether the Executive's absence from or inability to perform his duties hereunder was caused through incapacity, the certificate of any two registered medical practitioners, one to be appointed on behalf of the Executive and the other to be appointed on behalf of the Company (or in default of agreement between such practitioners, the certificate of an independent medical practitioner to be appointed by the President for the time being of the British Medical Association), shall be final and binding upon the parties. [The problem arises when an employee is away for a long time but the employer cannot be sure whether or not he or she is malingering. This clause is an attempt to resolve the problem.]

11. The Executive shall on the termination of his employment hereunder give notice resigning forthwith from all appointments he may hold as a Director of the Company or any Company in the Group. In the event of notice not being given within seven days of the termination of the Executive's employment, the Secretary of the Company (whom the Executive hereby appoints his Attorney for such purposes) shall give notice on his behalf. Upon termination the Executive shall immediately deliver up to the Company all property belonging to the Company or the Group which is in his possession or under his control. [If the Executive leaves or is dismissed he or she will have to be removed from any directorship held. He/she could be removed in the last resort by a shareholders' meeting; that, though, is obviously undesirable. This provision allows the Company secretary to give notice on behalf of the Executive. This power could not be used if the problem had been created by the

Executive's mental condition. If the Executive has become mentally unable to manage his/her affairs, consult your lawyer.]

12. On the termination of this Agreement for any cause the Executive shall not either on his own account or for any other person, firm or company for a period of three years from the date of such termination:

   (a) be engaged directly or indirectly in any business competing with or likely to compete with the business of the Company or any Company which is a member of the Group and which is situated within twenty-five miles from any branch office of any member of the Group.

   (b) solicit, interfere with or endeavour to entice away from any member of the Group any person, firm or company who was a customer or a client of the Company or a member of the Group during the year preceding the date of such termination.

   (c) employ or endeavour to entice away from the Company any person who was at the date of termination or within twelve months prior thereto in the employment of the Company or a member of the Group.

   (d) directly or indirectly interfere or seek to interfere with the continuance of supplies to the Company or any member of the Group from any supplier of goods or services to the Group during the twelve months preceding such termination.

   [Clause 12 is fraught with difficulties. Restraints of this nature are the subject of Chapter 4.]

13. Any notice given under this Agreement shall be deemed well served if (when addressed to the Company) it is left at or sent by first class recorded delivery addressed to the Company to its registered office or if (when addressed to the Executive) it is served personally or is sent by first class recorded delivery addressed to him at his usual or last known place of residence in England. In the case of post the day of service shall (unless the contrary shall be proved) be deemed to be two days after the date of posting.

14. The Appendices form part of this Agreement.

15. If any provision of this Agreement shall be found by any Court or Authority of competent jurisdiction to be invalid or unenforceable, such invalidity or unenforceability shall not affect the

remaining provisions of the Agreement which shall remain in force and effect. [The problem when some clause is found to be invalid is that it may mean that the whole agreement is invalid. Lawyers provide this clause in an attempt to prevent that being the case. The effect is that the agreement is then read as if the invalid clause had not been included. That is satisfactory, so long as the offending clause does not have an impact on the rest of the agreement. The usual problem arises on the clause that restricts competition after the employment has ended. That is the clause that is most likely to be rejected by the Court. In this agreement, the exclusion of that clause would not affect the rest of the agreement which would remain enforceable. So an act in breach of the duty of confidentiality, for example, could still be attacked by the employer.]

IN WITNESS whereof the parties hereto have executed these presents the day and year first above written.

Appendix 1: Definitions

Expression	Meaning
'The Directors'	The Directors of the Company for the time being
'The Board'	The Board of Directors of the Company for the time being
'The Group'	The Company, its ultimate holding company, any other company which is a subsidiary of such ultimate holding company and any associated company of any of them
'Holding Company'	The meanings attributed to that expression by Section 736 of the Companies Act 1985
'Subsidiary Company'	The meaning attributed to that expression by Section 736 of the Companies act 1985
'Associated Company'	The meaning attributed to that expression by Section 416 of the Income and Corporation Taxes Act 1988
'Appointment'	The appointment of the Executive in accordance with clause 2 as extended or varied from time to time

Appendix 2: Statutory information

For the purposes of the legislation in force at the date of this Agreement, the Executive is given the following information which may be varied from time to time:

Pension	There is no pension scheme in which the Executive can participate by virtue of his employment hereunder. Accordingly, notice is hereby given that a contracting out certificate is not at present in force in respect of his employment.
Normal hours of work	The Executive's normal hours of work are 9 a.m. to 5 p.m. Monday to Friday inclusive. The Executive acknowledges that the seniority of his position and the demands of the Company's business will frequently require additional time to be spent on the Company's business and acknowledges that no additional remuneration is payable in respect of such additional work.
Trade unions	The Executive has the right to belong to a trade union, including the right to participate in its activities and to become an officer thereof. The Executive also has the right not to belong to a trade union.
Continuous employment	No employment with a previous employer counts as a part of the Executive's period of previous employment.
Grievance procedure	Should the Executive have any grievance relating to his employment hereunder he should give notice in writing to the Company Secretary setting out the details of such grievance and if so required by the Executive the Secretary will refer the grievance to the next Board meeting of the Company. The Board's decision in relation to such grievance shall be final and binding and shall be communicated to the Executive in writing.
Disciplinary rules	By reason of the seniority of his position there are no specific disciplinary rules or procedures applicable to him other than those stated in this Agreement.

1.6 Changes in terms of employment of contractor

It is probably inevitable that over the period of a business life, changes will have to be made in the terms under which those engaged to perform work for the business are operating. If the contract is an ordinary employment contract (Letter 1 or Document 3, for example) then any attempt to change terms can become difficult. Whether the contract is an employment contract of service or whether it is a contract with some independent contractor to supply services, first of all the existing contract has to be ended and a new contract entered into. In the case of a contract for services (such as Letter 1) a notice will have to be given in accordance with the terms of the contract, or the two parties can simply agree to a variation. Letter 4 is a letter that could be written to bring this about.

Letter 4

Letter varying terms of employment

Dear

This is to record the agreement that we have now reached for a variation in the terms of your contract to supply a repair and maintenance service for us.

1. We have taken additional working space and the work that will fall to be done by you will inevitably increase. To recognise this we will increase your retainer to £18,000 per annum.
2. Because you will need to have help to carry out the additional work, we will pay an additional sum of £5,000 per annum to meet the extra cost that you will have to bear.

Please confirm your agreement to these changes by signing and returning one copy of this letter.

Yours sincerely

1.7 Change in terms of an employment contract

If the contract is a contract of service such as Letter 2 or Document 2, the employer cannot arbitrarily, in law, change the terms of employment. If the employee does not agree to a change, the employer must first bring the original contract to an end (by giving the appropriate notice) and then offer new employment on the revised terms and conditions. If the employer does this, or attempts to impose changes in contravention of the terms of the existing contract then the employee – provided that the qualifying service allows – can claim 'constructive dismissal' and apply to a Tribunal for compensation. This will be explained more fully in Chapter 6. A works meeting could be held at which the new terms are explained – this would probably be good personnel management, assuming that the alterations are non-contentious, for example they are brought about through a change in ownership and the new owner wants to bring the terms and conditions into line with the other contracts in force in the Group. A letter in the form of Letter 5 could be written.

Letter 5

Notice of proposed change in terms of employment

As all employees will be aware, John Smith (1985) Limited is now part of The Brown Organisation. So that all employees in the Group enjoy the same terms of employment, it is necessary to make certain changes in your terms of employment. We propose to bring these new conditions into effect in four weeks' time, and I enclose for you a copy of the new terms. I do not think that any of these changes are controversial, indeed I think that some of them are a distinct improvement on the old terms. I hope that they are easy to understand.

If you have any question or objections to these new terms, please discuss them with Mr Jones and I am sure that he will be able to explain the need for them and reassure you.

CHAPTER 2

Recruiting employees

The first step in formulating the employer/employee relationship is the recruitment of the employee for the work required to be done on the employer's behalf. The work might be of a simplistic nature, such as unskilled labouring on a building site or a general purpose worker in an office or a shop floor of a factory; or it might require a semi-skilled, skilled or a highly skilled person. In either case the advertising of the position available should be properly set out in line with the requirements – clearly indicating the expectations of the advertiser. The job specification should be succinctly expressed – even in the most simple of advertisements.

Advertisement 1

Advertisement for an unskilled employee

FACTORY CLEANERS WANTED

Cleaners wanted by John Smith Limited for their factory at Burgh Works, Newtown. Male or female. The work entails cleaning on the factory floor and in the offices. Hours of work from 7 p.m. to 10 p.m. Monday to Friday. Preference given to applicants willing to work on occasional Saturdays and Bank Holidays, for which payment at higher rates is made. Pay £7 per hour (normal), £9 per hour for weekend and holiday working. Apply to: Personnel Department, John Smith Limited, Burgh Works, Newtown.

In more sophisticated employment offers, an in-depth explanation of the job content would be required.

Advertisement 2

Advertisement for computer programmer

PROGRAMMERS TO INDUSTRY LIMITED

Our rapidly expanding Financial Services Division requires an additional programmer to write, design and test new programmes to meet the demands of investors, insurers, dealers and brokers. The successful applicant will, in addition, be required to review and update existing programmes and work as a member of an innovative team of programmers. The successful applicant will be a graduate with at least four years' experience. A salary in the range of £20,000 to £25,000 is offered, with generous benefit package including car, non-contributory pension and insurance, health insurance for the applicant and family, profit sharing scheme and assistance with relocation expenses. Write with full CV to Clarinda James, Programmers to Industry Limited, Computer House, Duke Street, Newtown.

The advertisement should avoid any reference to race or sex, even when advertising specific jobs for specific groups. For example, a position arises for a social worker with a commitment to black families and their social problems and the person appointed would require specific skills for that area of social work. It would be presumptuous to assume that an applicant other than a black applicant would not be suitable; this would only be established at any subsequent interview, and it may be that an applicant of another racial background would be eminently suitable. The Race and Sex Discrimination Acts must be kept in mind when compiling advertisements for prospective employment – no matter what the employment may consist of.

Advertisement 3

Advertisement for welfare officer

WELFARE OFFICER

Johnson Conglomerates PLC require an experienced person to provide social and welfare services to its workforce. The Company employs a large number of workers from all ethnic groups. The successful applicant will need to show, in addition to detailed knowledge of social and welfare law and regulations, an understanding and sympathy for those of our workers who seek or are in need of help. Experience in working with families from the Afro-Caribbean ethnic group would be an advantage. Write with full CV to James Jackson, Personnel Department, Johnson Conglomerates PLC, Shaw Lane, Newtown.

The nature of the employment contract that is on offer should also be clearly indicated and should state whether the contract of service is an on-going one with an initial period of probationary employment requiring to be fulfilled, or a fixed term contract of employment with a definite beginning and a definite termination date. This will ensure that the prospective applicant will be in no doubt as to both the nature of the work requiring to be done and the contractual boundaries that he or she can expect.

Advertisement 4

Advertisement for position for a limited period

SECRETARY TO THE MANAGING DIRECTOR

A secretary is required for the Managing Director of John Smith Limited. His present secretary is on maternity leave and is expected to return to her duties in nine months' time. Whilst it would be hoped that the person appointed to be her temporary replacement could be found alternative employment when the present secretary returns, no guarantee can be given that a position will be available. The successful applicant will work flexi-hours with 11 a.m. to 3 p.m. as core hours. A salary of £12,000 p.a. plus season ticket loan and other benefits is offered. No shorthand but experience of word processing with Word Perfect necessary. Write with full CV to Miss B. Jones, John Smith Limited, 22 Park Lane, Newtown.

If the job required to be done would be within the physical capabilities of a disabled person, then this should be indicated in the advertisement in order that the widest possible selection of prospective applicants should be available, and also to ensure that the current labour market is being tapped to its fullest potential.

Advertisement 5

Advertisement to include disabled person

ACCOUNTS CLERK

Accounts clerk required. Experience of working with computerised accounting procedures essential. Our premises have been fully adapted to accommodate disabled persons and applications from persons suffering under a disability would be welcomed. Hours are from 9 a.m. to 5.30 p.m. Mondays to Fridays. Three weeks' holiday with pay in addition to statutory holidays. Salary £250 per week. Apply in writing to John Smith Limited, 22 Park Lane, Newtown.

Lastly, it should be noted that when advertising jobs that require the employment of children (that is, someone under the age of 16 years) and young persons (that is, someone between the ages of 16 and 18 years), this is expressed clearly in any advertisement or information that might be lodged with the various employment agencies or other recruiting areas. There are specific rules and regulations applying to the employment of these groups. The employment of a child under the age of 13 years is prohibited. Because working conditions for children and young persons are strictly controlled, care should be exercised in the compilation of any advertisement or of information letters seeking applicants for such employment.

Advertisement 6

Advertisement for a young person

JOHN SMITH LIMITED

We have a vacancy for a young person in our general office. The duties will be to assist the office manager in her duties, to deal with the opening and posting of the mail and to assist in the general work of the office. The successful applicant will be given the opportunity to study and to gain experience in all office procedures. Preference will be given to applicants with at least three GCSE passes. Hours of work are 9 a.m. to 5.30 p.m. Monday to Friday with one hour for lunch. Apply in own handwriting to Mrs M. Coach, John Smith Limited, 22 Park Lane, Newtown.

In all cases it is recommended that the advertiser either requests the applicant to provide a full curriculum vitae (CV), setting out brief details of his or her education and work experience, or offers 'employment application forms' to prospective applicants so as to gain maximum knowledge of the applicants and their possible capabilities before the short-listing process is undertaken. Where, as in all the forms of advertisement suggested in this chapter, a CV is requested, applicants who appear worthy of short-listing should be asked to complete an employment application form.

Document 3

Employment application form

1. Full name and address
2. Education
3. Previous employment over last ten years
4. Reason for leaving last employment
5. Any illnesses during the past five years which have resulted in more than three weeks' absence from work
6. Any permanent disability
7. Experience of [work process for which employment is sought]
8. Dependants

CHAPTER 3

Employees' statutory rights

3.1 Remuneration

The rights of both employer and employee are initially found in the contract between them. The law has, however, given the employee additional rights, whatever the contract may say. For example, the employee has the right, by statute, to a statement of the terms upon which he or she is employed. Such a statement is set out in Chapter 1 (Document 1). He or she also has the statutory right not to be dismissed unfairly and to receive a redundancy payment if made redundant. Both these rights are described in greater detail in Chapter 6.

So far as the wages are concerned, an employee is entitled to receive a statement showing his or her gross earnings less those deductions which are being made (for example for PAYE taxation and national insurance contributions) and the net amount payable. In the case of any deductions, these must include an indication of the purposes for which they are being made. It is an offence to fail to do so. Not only is it an offence but an employee who has been refused a PAYE slip can take his or her complaint to the industrial tribunal where the employer will be ordered to make a penalty payment, usually computed as the amount of the deductions that should have been shown had a pay statement been properly issued (limited to the last thirteen weeks immediately before application is made to the tribunal).

Document 4

Pay slip

John Smith Limited

Name of employee	Ronald Brown
Pay for week ended	5 October 1990

Hourly rate £7.15	Hours worked 40
Gross pay	£286.00
PAYE tax	£ 63.23
NIC	£ 25.00
Total tax and NIC	£ 88.23
Net	£197.77
Other deductions	
(see separate statement)	
Net pay	£197.77

The slip must show all proper deductions that have been made. The general rule is that all deductions are unlawful unless they have been required by law, provided for in the worker's contract of employment (in which case he or she must have had written details as, for example, in Letter 2) or, where they are not in the contract, where he/she has agreed to the deduction in writing before the deduction was made. Letter 6 is an acknowledgement by an employee of the right to deduct payments to repay a loan made by the employer.

Letter 6

Acknowledgement agreeing to deductions to repay a loan

To John Smith Limited

I acknowledge receipt of the sum of £125.00 advanced to me (free of interest) to enable me to purchase my monthly season ticket. I agree that I will use this advance solely for the purpose of purchasing a season ticket and I agree that there may be deducted from my weekly wages the sum of £31.25, the first of those deductions to be made on my next payday. In the event that I leave your employment before the whole of this loan has been repaid, then the whole of the amount which remains due may be deducted from any wages then due to me and any deficiency will be immediately repayable by me.

Caroline Jones

It may be that from time to time an employer might wish to make some deduction from an employee's wages or salary apart from the tax and national insurance contribution. For example, a deduction for a till shortfall or a penalty for lateness or an unauthorised absence. Such a deduction is unlawful unless there is written agreement by the employee to such deductions being made. Deductions for these matters are controlled. The law is quite specific on the matter of how much may be deducted from an employee's daily or weekly earnings. In the case of an employee in the retail trade deductions to cover cash shortages may not exceed one-tenth of the wages on any payday. There is an exception when an employee leaves, when any outstanding amount, without limit, can be deducted. 'Retail trade' for this purpose, covers all work where there is a supply of goods or services whether on a regular basis or not, and it includes rent collectors and other agents who call to collect regular payments – in effect, any employees dealing with third parties who receive money for sales or other transactions of their employers, the old-fashioned 'tallyman', for example. Where there is no written agreement such as Letter 2 and it is desired to take a right to deduct payments, then an agreement in writing signed by the employee must be obtained before any deduction is made.

Letter 7

Acknowledgement by employee of liability to have deductions made from wages

To John Smith Limited

I acknowledge that in my new duties of collector of payments for goods sold on mail order I will be receiving monies from customers for which I shall have to account at the end of each day. I agree that in the event that at the end of the week any shortages shall be discovered of monies which I should have collected and accounted for, those shortages may be deducted from my weekly wages up to the maximum from time to time permitted by law. (I understand that at the date of this acknowledgement the maximum amount is 10 per cent of the gross wages due to me.) If at the time I leave your employment there shall be any balance due, then the whole of that balance, without any limitation, may be deducted from any sums due to me. If those sums due to me are insufficient to repay the amount outstanding, then the balance will immediately be paid by me.

William Brown

In one instance, deductions can be made without the employee's agreement; that is the case of a deduction made under an attachment of earnings order. Such orders can be made as a manner of collecting a civil debt and are now being made to collect unpaid Poll Tax. The Court (usually the local County Court) orders the employer to make a regular deduction from wages. Under the Court machinery leading to the making of an order, the debtor is required to give a statement of his or her means and an enquiry is made as to the income he needs to live on. The Registrar will then fix what is called a 'protected earnings rate' which is the amount which should be left after all deductions. He or she then orders a 'normal deduction rate' which is the amount that is notified to the employer as the amount to be deducted. This amount will have to appear on the pay slip (Document 4). In this case, as the deduction will be a regular standing deduction, it can be shown as a total sum without any explanation, so long as the employee is given a statement of the nature of the deduction at least once every twelve months.

Letter 8

Letter notifying an employee of deductions

To William Brown

We have received from Oxford County Court an Order that we must deduct from your weekly wages the sum of £15. As a result, you will see on each weekly pay slip an amount, in the space following the words 'other deductions', of £15. This deduction will continue until the order is discharged.

For John Smith Limited

When an employee against whom an attachment of earnings order has been made leaves employment, the employer is under a duty to notify the Court and, if known, tell the Court the name and address of the new employer.

Letter 9

Letter notifying the Court of ending of employment

The Chief Clerk,
Oxford County Court,
Court Offices,
Oxford

Dear Sir

re William Brown, attachment of earnings order no. 1234

We have to inform you that William Brown, in respect of whom the above attachment of earnings order was made, left our employment last Friday 31 August.

We understand that he is now employed by Joseph Williams Limited of Burgh Works, Newtown, Staffordshire.

Yours faithfully

In the same way, when an employee who is known to be under an attachment of earnings order joins the business, it is under a duty to notify the Court which made the order.

Letter 10

Letter informing the Court of employment of an employee subject to an attachment of earnings order

The Chief Clerk,
Oxford County Court,
Court Offices,
Oxford

Dear Sir

re William Brown, attachment of earnings order

On 3 September, the above named, formerly employed by John Smith Limited, was employed by us as a rent collector. We have been informed by John Smith Limited that an attachment of earnings order exists against Brown under which they had been deducting the sum of £15 per week.

Brown's weekly wage will be the sum of £250 from which there will be deducted the PAYE and NIC payments due from him and in addition he has agreed under his terms of employment with us that we may deduct from his weekly wages any deficiences that may be found in the monies due to be collected by him.

Please acknowledge receipt of this letter.

Yours faithfully

The method of payment of the wage or salary was, at one time, regulated by law and it was unlawful to make any payment except in coin of the realm. However, the previous Acts of Parliament which made these laws were repealed by the Wages Act 1986. This does not affect any contractual agreement that might exist between the employer and the employee as to method of payment, only that the statutory right to payment by 'cash' has disappeared. The increasing use of banking facilities by far more workers has meant that, in the main, the employee will probably be expected to accept a contractual provision as to cheque payments rather than cash – indeed, most monthly salaried employees will have been paid this way for many years. If the contract of employment stipulates that the employee can expect to be paid weekly in cash, and there is an attempt unilaterally to change this provision to a cheque payment, then (at least in law) the employee can claim that the contract has been breached by the employer and claim constructive dismissal before the industrial tribunal. Whilst such a course of action is unlikely, no chance should be given. A letter (a modification of Letter 4) could be written.

Letter 11

Memo introducing payment of wages by cheque

Dear

We are increasingly concerned over the risks to our cashiers when they collect the large amounts of cash from the bank each Friday.

We have decided that in the interests of security, in future payment of wages should be by cheque instead of cash. Would you please complete the tear-off slip at the end of this memo and give it to the wages office.

For any employees who do not have a bank account, we have made arrangements with our bank (Newbury Bank PLC) under which any employee may open an account. So long as the account remains in credit no charges will be made.

If you object to this change, please notify the wages office by Friday of next week.

We propose to bring these new conditions into effect in four weeks' time, which will give time for those who do not have an account to make the necessary arrangements with Newbury Bank PLC.

If you have any questions on this proposal please discuss them with Mr Jones in the wages office and I am sure that he will be able to explain the need for them and reassure you.

Personnel Officer

I agree to accept payment by cheque.
My bank is   at   branch. The Bank sort code is and account number is

---

It may happen that an employer finds him- or herself in a position where it is necessary to adopt short-time working. Trade has declined but it is thought that the recession is of a temporary nature and rather than make a valuable workforce redundant, employees are asked to work short time or possibly not be provided with work on a normal working day. The law provides that in these circumstances employees with at least one month's continuous service shall be guaranteed a basic payment. The payment is based upon their normal daily pay but not exceeding £11.30 per day nor exceeding five days in any period of three months. An employee will lose this right if he or she refuses alternative work which, although not within the terms of his or her contract, is suitable in the circumstances. Where an employee takes this action, then Letter 8 should be written. The point is that if an employer fails to pay the guaranteed wage, the employee can complain to the industrial tribunal. On such a complaint, the employer will want to show that he or she has offered suitable alternative work which has been refused.

Letter 12

Offer of alternative work in lieu of short-time work

Dear

You are aware that in the present economic conditions we have been forced to consider short-time working. In your job as driver of our short distance delivery vans, falling orders have meant that temporarily there is insufficient work for you. We have offered you the alternative work of driver for the Managing Director but you have refused to undertake these duties.

In these circumstances you are not entitled to the statutory guaranteed wage and you will not therefore receive any payment during those days when we have no work to offer you in your normal job.

Personnel Officer

There can be occasions when health and safety regulations demand than an employee be suspended from work because of a health hazard. In such cases the employee who has served at least one month's continuous service may be entitled to be paid during the period of suspension. As in the case of short-time working, an employee who refuses to accept suitable alternative work will lose his or her right to this payment. As in that case also, the employee has the right to complain to an industrial tribunal if payment is wrongfully withheld. A letter in similar terms to Letter 12 should be written, although obviously it will refer to the medical condition that has made suspension necessary. Whilst the employee is suspended, a replacement can be engaged on terms that his or her employment will be liable to end when the disabled employee again becomes fit to resume his or her duties. To have the advantage of creating an employment of this nature which can be determined for no reason connected with the employee, it is necessary that the employee is informed in writing at the time of the engagement that this possibility exists. Letter 3 gives the appropriate information.

3.2 Sickness

In modern employment, absenteeism through ill-health, either short- or long-term, has become a major factor in working hours lost. The increasing stress of life in general, added to the greater demands being made in the more competitive world of work, are the major factors that now affect the general pattern of attendance at work. There is no doubt at all that many employers find their businesses adversely affected by varying degrees of absenteeism.

The question of paying the employee for his or her periods of absence through ill-health now rests with the employer under the social security legislation now known as ESSP (Employee's Statutory Sick Pay).

The ESSP scheme requires the employer to pay the employee sickness entitlement as laid down in the tables of rates applicable. The employer may choose to pay sickness benefit at a rate over and above the statutory rate, but cannot reclaim the excess. Further, to enable the employer to recover the ESSP the employer would have to apply the rules of the scheme correctly and follow the guidelines as laid down in the various pamphlets available that cover the operation of the scheme.

The employee's right, briefly stated, is to be paid when:

(a) he or she has been sick for at least four consecutive days (including Sundays and public holidays); and
(b) he or she has told the employer of his/her sickness; and
(c) he or she has given evidence of sickness to the employer.

An employer who finds an employee absent without having complied with these conditions should write Letter 13. It is important that copies should be retained of certificates given by the employee's doctor. A record should be kept of his or her name and address in case it becomes necessary to contact him/her for verification of the nature of the illness and probable length of time before the employee will be available for work.

Letter 13

Letter to absent employee

Dear

I am given to understand that you are unable to come to work because you are unwell. I do not know whether or not this is correct. You have not contacted us nor given any medical certificate of your sickness.

I remind you that under the terms of your employment, you are entitled to be paid whilst absent through sickness but must account to us for the amount of any sickness benefit to which you are entitled. You are only entitled to benefit if we are notified of your illness and given some evidence of your incapacity for work.

Unless I hear from you, I must assume that your absence is not due to sickness. If you are unwell but choose not to claim sickness benefit it is right that you should know that the amount of the benefit to which you would otherwise be entitled will be deducted from your pay.

You are in any event only entitled to pay for four weeks of sickness.

Yours sincerely

Many employers do have in-house agreements in which the employee, dependent upon his or her service, will have the benefit of being paid the normal week's or month's wages without any deduction even though he or she is off sick; sometimes this can be a graduated number of weeks at full and half pay. Any arrangement as to pay during sickness must be referred to in the contract of employment, or letter of appointment (if either of these documents apply — see Letter 2 and Document 2). It must also be referred to in the statement of terms (see Document 1).

The period of the employer's responsibility for ESSP is set at twenty-eight weeks. At the end of that time, if the employee is still unable to return to work, he or she would then have to submit the medical certification to the local office of the Department of Health and Social Security. The employer will still wish to be informed of the position because the question will have to be faced whether or not the employment can or should be ended. The normal law of contract applies to a contract of employment. It is modified only by the right of the employee not to have that contract ended unfairly. A contract can end where performance is 'frustrated'. The industrial tribunals have had to consider the circumstances of frustration of a contract of employment on more than one occasion. In one case, eighteen months' absence sick was held not to frustrate the contract, in another four months was held sufficient. It all depends upon the facts. The employer must follow certain basic steps in the termination procedure so as to provide both a proper standard of reasonableness and equity and be able to offer a sound defence should the dismissed employee take his or her case to the industrial tribunal.

The first step in the procedure is to establish that the employee is sick and that certification is correct, and supported by the employee's doctor. In most formal contracts of employment there will be a clause entitling the employer to medical confirmation of the employee's sickness (see, for example, the provisions in Document 2). Letter 13 above is a form of letter that would be written at the commencement of absence. In the case of prolonged absence Letter 14 could be written.

Letter 14

Letter to an employee after long absence through sickness

Dear

I am very sorry to see that you are still unwell and unable to return to work. I will need to have an opinion from your doctor as to the probable length of time that it will be before you will be able to return to work. Could you please sign and return to me the enclosed letter. I have your doctor's name and address from the medical certificates that he has supplied in the past.

Yours sincerely

Personnel Officer

Enclosure:
Dr W. Kildair
The Surgery
Main Street
Newtown

Dear Dr Kildair

My employers, John Smith Limited, will be writing to you about my illness and the fact that I am unable to work.

Will you please answer such questions as they may ask about my illness and any matters that relate to it and to my likely period of absence from work in the future. They will be responsible for any fees that you may charge in this connection.

Yours sincerely

The next step would depend upon the job that the employee was employed to do and the necessity of filling the post on a temporary basis whilst the employee remained away from work. It might be that the employee can be carried on the sick list for quite some time before the question of either a replacement or termination is to be considered. On the other hand, the employee might have a poor record of attendance over a period of time, and the question is raised in the employer's mind as to the veracity of the employee, and the possibility that he or she is malingering. The reply from the employee's doctor may satisfy these concerns. If they do not, the question of a second opinion has to be considered. All communication with the employee should avoid reference to misconduct or threats of disciplinary action, because, until it is fairly established that the reason for absence is not reasonably justified, the reasons given must be accepted. Letter 15 could be written where the employer remains unsatisfied after hearing from the employee's own doctor.

Letter 15

Letter requesting second medical opinion

Dear

I have heard from your doctor following the authority you gave to me. In the light of what he has said I would like to have a second opinion on your condition.

I would ask if you would allow Dr Finlay (the Company's medical consultant) to see you at our expense so that we may have the benefit of his advice.

Yours sincerely

Personnel Officer

If as a result of careful investigation the employer decides that there is no alternative and that the employment must be terminated, the employer must take the course of action described in Chapter 6 on unfair dismissal.

3.3 Pregnancy

One other reason for absence through health matters – though not to be associated with the general area of sickness and its treatment, except in particular cases – is the question of pregnancy and the consequent maternity leave entitlement as laid down in the statute. The main point to note is that the employee will have had to complete two years' continuous service with the employer prior to the eleventh week before the expected week of confinement if she is to qualify for the provisions related to maternity leave and the right to return to work. There is a further complication for the woman who is employed by an employer who has less than six employees – the Employment Act 1980 'Exclusion of Small Firms' provision. In general, however, it will be potentially an unfair dismissal should a worker be dismissed on grounds related to her pregnancy. More important still is the fact that the onus of proof lies on the employer as to the real reason for the dismissal should a pregnant woman have been dismissed and claim that she holds the reasonable belief that she has been dismissed for reasons related to her condition. A considerable problem exists for an employer who has an unsatisfactory female employee who he or she was proposing to dismiss for proper reasons but who then announces her pregnancy. Chapter 6 suggests a series of letters to be written before actually ending the employment. If the employer has, before the announcement of the pregnancy, written one or more letters of the type recommended in Chapter 6, hope exists that it will be possible to provide the heavy burden of proof that is necessary.

It is recommended that the employer should tell the expectant mother as soon as possible of her rights to maternity leave and to return to work. As in all these matters, with one eye on the possibilities of an application to an industrial tribunal it is best that these things are recorded in writing. Letter 16 is the sort of letter to write. In this instance the letter has been drafted in a friendly fashion to suit the sort of relationship that one could imagine exists in the circumstances of Advertisement 4. If that degree of informality is inappropriate, then a letter giving the same information but omitting the social niceties can be written.

Letter 16

To a pregnant employee

Dear

Thank you for telling us of the news of your pregnancy. I do hope that all goes well for you. You probably know that you have the right to time off with pay to attend any ante-natal clinic and that you have the right to statutory maternity pay. In case you are not sure about this, let me explain. If you are still pregnant at the eleventh week before your expected confinement and have then (or after then) ceased work because of your pregnancy, you are entitled to the payment. The payment is made by us. The conditions made by the DSS to govern this right require you to give medical evidence of the date of your expected confinement and that you give us at least twenty-one days notice before you leave for the confinement. You are entitled to say that you intend to return to work after the baby is born. As I am sure you will understand, it is going to be necessary for us to cover the work during your absence. So if you intend to return, please let me know as soon as possible. I would prefer it that you gave me this information in writing. I am sorry to be formal about this but this is one time when formality is necessary. If you decide later to change your mind and stay at home, you are absolutely free to do so without any problems for you. If after the baby is born you decide that you will be coming back, it will be necessary for you to write and let me know the day on which you will return as soon as you can give a precise date.

If you have any questions on any of your rights, please let me know and I will try to help.

Yours sincerely

As Letter 16 indicates, the pregnant woman has the right to time off with pay for ante-natal care (another example of the guaranteed payment rights referred to above) but to entitle her to this benefit she must, if the employer requests it, produce a medical certificate confirming her pregnancy, plus an appointment card or some other evidence of her attendance at the ante-natal clinic or wherever it is she has her appointment. Letter 16, it will be noticed, has called for the production of medical evidence of pregnancy in what, it is hoped, is a tactful way. If this letter has not been written, there is always the possibility that the employee might complain, either that she was not allowed time off or that she was not given the pay to which she was entitled. To cover that possibility, Letter 17 could be written.

Letter 17

Request for evidence of attendance at an ante-natal appointment

Dear

This is to confirm that you are entitled be paid during any attendance at an ante-natal clinic or any other ante-natal appointment that you have to keep during your pregnancy. Will you please ask your doctor to let us have a certificate confirming that you are pregnant and please, so that we can make appropriate arrangements, give us as much advance notice as possible on each occasion that you have to attend an ante-natal appointment. For the purposes of our records we shall also want to see the appointment card of your attendances at the clinic.

Yours sincerely

Letter 16 also refers to the fact that the pregnant employee has the right to the preservation of her employment. This is a right that exists both during, and for a period to twenty-nine weeks after, the end of her pregnancy. She must inform her employer at least three weeks before she leaves for her confinement that she is going to be away and that she expects to return to work. She need not give this in writing, unless the employer requests it. In the case of an emergency where she has no opportunity to give the notice, she must give it as soon as reasonably practical. Then she has to notify her employer seven days in advance of her actual return that she is returning. She can, of course, even though she gave notice of her intention to return, change her mind without telling her employer. The employer will, of course, be in a position to hire a temporary replacement so long as that replacement is left in no doubt that the job is 'temporary' and not an offer of continuous employment. Advertisement 4 is an indication of the sort of advertisement which should be used to engage a replacement. A letter along the lines of Letter 3 should be written to the replacement. Letter 18 is a suggested form to use.

Letter 18

On engaging a replacement for an employee absent on maternity leave

Dear

I confirm the offer made to you of employment as secretary to our Managing Director on the terms discussed and set out in the enclosed memorandum.

As I told you at the interview, the vacancy has occurred because of the absence, on maternity leave, of Mr Smith's permanent secretary. She has expressed an intention to return to work at the end of her confinement and if she does return in accordance with this intention, I fear that there will be no other position to offer to you and your engagement will then be terminated.

I look forward to seeing you on Monday morning and hope that you will enjoy working with us.

Yours sincerely

The employer is in the difficult position of not knowing whether or not the absent employee will or will not return. If she does, the replacement will have to be discharged; if she does not, the replacement will have to be asked to stay. The absent employee has twenty-nine weeks from the week of her confinement to exercise this right of return. To protect the employer it is provided that if the employer requests it she must confirm her intention to return in writing. The employer's request must be made not earlier than forty-nine days after the week of the confinement and the employee must reply within fourteen days. If she does not reply within this time she loses the right. Letter 19 is an appropriate letter to write in these circumstances.

Letter 19

To returning employee after confinement

Dear

When you left to have your baby you said that you intended to return to work. Can you now please confirm to me in writing whether this is still your intention and say when you expect to return. You will understand that I have to consider the position of the replacement I engaged to do your work whilst you were away.

It is right that I should tell you that unless you reply to this letter within fourteen days telling me of your intentions, you will lose your legal right to return.

Yours sincerely

3.4 Trade union activity

There are other regulated periods of activity that the employer may have to recognise, should circumstances require that recognition. In the event that a trade union recognition agreement exists between the employer's organisation and the relevant trade union or unions, then there may well be elected trade union officials within the employer's workforce. These could be shop stewards, safety representatives, convenors of numerous trade unions within the organisation, and works committees. These elected officials are entitled to reasonable time off with pay for specific union/industrial relations/employee and employer matters. There are basic premises to be observed: the union duties must relate to the employer/employee in-house relationship, and not to matters that are extraneous to the employment, such as political meetings and trade union matters that are related to general industrial relations (unless there is a direct connection between these general matters and the direct employment, such as a national joint council meeting that covers the industry from which the shop steward or safety representative comes). In the main, the time off should be an agreed period between the union and the employer and related to the requirements of the organisation's functions. The employer should ensure that the time off requested should be for the purpose that is stated. Should any abuse of the procedure become apparent, then the union would have to discipline its own members and officials in line with the recognition agreement that exists with the employer. Clearly, in the interests of good employer–employee relations no employer would wish to provoke a confrontation with the union and before any letter is written an informal discussion of problems would take place. Where the situation deteriorates to the point that some more formal complaint becomes appropriate, Letter 20 could be written.

Letter 20

Letter to a trade union complaining of an abuse of privileges by a shop steward

The Secretary,
T&GU

Dear

I am very sorry that I have to make a formal approach to you about James Wood. I have mentioned to you informally that I had evidence that he was using his union activities as an excuse to take unauthorised absences from work.

Yesterday, he informed me that he was to attend a meeting of shop stewards from other works in this county to discuss matters relating to safety and conditions of work in the industry. In accordance with our standing arrangements, time off with pay was sanctioned for this meeting. I have now heard from others who attended the meeting that Wood was not there. I asked him for an explanation but he refuses to give any reason for his non-attendance and insists on his rights to be absent.

He is clearly using his union office as an excuse for absenteeism. If this continues, I will be left with no alternative but to take disciplinary action against him. I do not want to disturb the good relations that we have always enjoyed with the union and ask that you investigate the matter and take appropriate action to ensure that this abuse of union representation is brought to an end.

Yours sincerely

Time off for the recognised trade union safety representative is, however, another matter altogether. The Health and Safety at Work Act 1974 requires the employer who is within a recognition agreement with the appropriate trade union to allow a certain amount of reasonable time off with pay so as to enable the safety representative who has been elected and appointed by the recognised trade union to carry out his or her duties under the Act. These will be explained in Chapter 5. An employer refusing to allow a reasonable amount of time off under these provisions could be the subject of a complaint to an industrial tribunal. The amount of time allowed is no more than is reasonable. If an unreasonable amount of time were taken then the employer might have an answer to the complaint. Before refusing to give time off, though, the employer should see that he or she has, by writing a letter such as letter 21, some evidence that can be brought before the tribunal to establish the reasonableness of his or her actions.

Letter 21

Letter warning that an unreasonable amount of time off is being taken

Dear

Safety at work meetings

As you know, I have always been ready and willing to accede to your requests for time off to attend to your duties as the union safety representative. The amount of time that you are demanding on this account is now becoming unreasonable. In the past month you have taken five whole days for meetings and on five other days you have taken time away from your place of work. On two of those days you were away for two hours each time and on two others for one hour. On the fifth of those days you left at 2.30 p.m. and did not return to work that day.

I cannot accept that this is reasonable and must ask you to curtail the amount of time you are devoting to these matters. Unless you do I shall, reluctantly, have to consider refusing requests for absence.

Yours sincerely

3.5 Public duties

Where public duties are concerned, many employers do grant time off with pay for the employee who may be a local councillor or a justice of the peace. This is not a legal requirement and is a matter for negotiation between employee and employer. Where there is some arrangement reached, it is best that it is recorded in writing and Letter 22 is suggested.

Letter 22

Letter giving sanction to time off for public duties

Dear

I congratulate you on your success in the recent local elections and for the sake of good order, I confirm that I will permit you to take time off with pay to perform your duties as local councillor.

I am sure that you would not abuse this concession. In fairness to the company, though, I must make the reservation that the amount of time off be kept within reasonable limits and above all must not be allowed to grow to such an extent as will prevent you fulfilling your duties here. I know that you will understand why I have to make this formal point. As I have said, I have confidence in your integrity and can rely upon you.

Yours sincerely

3.6 Disciplinary code

The contract of employment and the statement of particulars will contain clauses related to discipline and its procedures. The cautious employer will ensure not only that these procedures are clearly established but that all the employees in the organisation are made fully aware of them.

If any organisation is to run effectively, then there has to be a system of rules and discipline so as to ensure that the employee knows the boundaries of his or her behaviour at work and what will be regarded as acceptable behaviour and what will lead to disciplinary action being taken. The rules and procedure should set out who is responsible for implementing the disciplinary procedure and what sanctions would be available to that person should those rules be transgressed. Appendix A gives a draft of a code of practice and disciplinary procedure that could be adopted. To ensure that employees cannot plead that they were not aware of this code, a copy should be given to each employee on joining the company. As it is only human nature to forget these things and to mislay documents, it is as well that, from time to time, a reminder is put into the wages envelope. Letter 23 is such a reminder.

Letter 23

Reminder of disciplinary code

All employees are reminded of the code of practice and disciplinary procedures in force in this Company. A copy of the code was given to every employee on joining the Company. If you have mislaid your copy of the code a further copy can be obtained from the Personnel Office

---

It is well established in unfair dismissal case law that the employer's rules of procedure and enforcement of sanctions and punitive measures against an employee who transgresses those rules must be both fairly and equitably set out and imposed.

Failure to warn or consult with erring employees may very well lead to a finding of unfair dismissal or constructive dismissal being made against an employer who has embarked on a disciplinary measure without an acceptable procedure being operated. Fines or deductions from wages; demotion from a particular post held for disciplinary reasons; suspension without pay for a defined period as a disciplinary sanction; warnings and reprimands without a proper procedure for issuing the same; the availability of appeal procedures to an employee who has been disciplined at work; removal from one job to another by reason of incapability or incompetence without a reasonable procedure being in operation so as to enable the employee an opportunity to improve – all these are measures that can be fraught with problems for the employer in the event that the employer has failed to set up even the most basic of procedures – no matter how many employees there are in the organisation, even where there are only one or two. As in every case where there is a possibility that a complaint may be made to a tribunal, it is best for the employer to see that he or she has recorded the position in writing. Before taking disciplinary action give at least one warning in writing (when it comes to a case of dismissal, as will be made clear in Chapter 6, more than one warning should definitely be given). Letter 24 is a first warning of possible discipline; Letter 25 is a follow-up.

Letter 24

Warning of possible disciplinary action

Dear

You have already been warned that your continued bad time keeping cannot be tolerated. I remind you that the Company's code of conduct, of which you have a copy, refers expressly to 'bad time keeping' as an instance of unsatisfactory conduct. Twice last week, and again yesterday, you were more than one hour late for work. I remind you that your hours are from 9 a.m. to 5.30 p.m.

This letter is a formal written warning given to you under the code of discipline and it has been recorded on your record card. If your time keeping does not improve you will be liable to dismissal.

If you consider that this warning is unfair, I remind you of your rights of appeal under the disciplinary code. In case you have mislaid your copy of the code, a further copy is enclosed.

Yours sincerely

Personnel Manager

Letter 25

Second warning of breach of discipline

Dear

You have had more than one oral warning of your bad time keeping and on 1 October I wrote to you with a formal written warning.

Despite these warnings your time keeping remains unsatisfactory. Twice last week, on Monday and again yesterday, you were over an hour late for work. This is the last formal warning you will be given. Any further lateness will result in your dismissal.

I remind you again of your rights of appeal if you consider that this warning is unfair.

Yours sincerely

Personnel Manager

3.7 ACAS

In large and middle-sized businesses the main controller of disputes over such matters as unfair procedures, threat by employees or unions of industrial action and similar matters is the Advisory Conciliation and Arbitration Service (ACAS for short).

Many industrial relations problems, even in small organisations, can often be resolved by the various parties concerned in the dispute getting round the table to try to resolve their differences. All disciplinary procedures – union or non-union –

should incorporate an ultimate clause relating either to internal conciliation, appeals and a disputes procedure, or a reference to the fact that the dispute will be referred to ACAS should there be a failure to agree. ACAS is available as an advisory service to all in British industry, whether trade unions, employers' associations or just individuals requiring advice. It is not permitted to take up a particular case or problem for a client but only to advise. Should the problem relate to a potentially unfair dismissal, then the ACAS official can certainly indicate to either party his views on the relative merits of the claim or defence, but this has to take the form of impartial advice. As far as other areas of industrial relations are concerned, the ACAS officer will often be in the best position to bring about a meeting of minds between the parties to the dispute.

The preparation of the rules and grievance procedures – encompassing the disciplinary rules of the particular organisation – can be a major task for the small and medium-sized company. It should be emphasised again that a lack of procedure will almost certainly lead to future problems for the employer who has failed to prepare these systems adequately. ACAS is always available for assistance in these matters, and has its own 'code of practice' on disciplinary procedures. These codes of practice do not carry statutory weight before the industrial tribunals, but they are recognised as 'good practice'. The code of practice in Appendix A has been based upon the ACAS code as adapted for the small and middle-sized business.

CHAPTER 4

Employees' duties

4.1 Loyalty

Once the employee has agreed the terms and conditions of the contract, he or she assumes obligations and duties to the employer and a failure to observe them is a breach of those contract terms. It may be that some matters are not specifically set out in the contract; nevertheless, so long as the relationship exists, there will be an implied duty of loyalty to the employer, in all matters that relate to the employment offered and accepted. The average contract of employment may not specify all the matters that the law implies and it would not be unusual if the basic premise that the employee would render faithful service was not spelled out in so many words. However, the implication of faithful service is an integral part of the relationship. In Document 2, clause 3(a) specifically states this obligation whilst Letter 3 does not. An employee engaged under either basis would have the same obligation. This duty means that the employee must promote the employer's interests over his or her own. The employee may be tempted when learning of a business opportunity to exploit it for personal gain. For example, if a surveyor employed by a property developer finds a development opportunity which he or she would like to exploit for him- or herself, this is not permitted. If the surveyor does exploit the opportunity, he or she will be in breach of contract and could be liable to account to the employer for any profits made as well as render him- or herself liable to dismissal. Letter 26 is the warning letter to an employee who might be tempted.

Letter 26

Letter drawing attention to duty of loyalty

Dear

I was disappointed to learn that you had been told of the fact that the land at Blackacre had been given planning consent for development and that instead of informing me of that fact and that the owner was inviting offers for its purchase, you discussed the matter with Jones and Partners. I hope you had in mind some advantage that you were going to offer to this Company. In giving you the benefit of the doubt as to your motives, let me make clear that you have a duty of loyalty to the Company and that this loyalty must be given priority over any other lawful considerations. I am putting this in writing as I feel that the matter is so important that a formal record should exist. When you have considered what I have said, I would like to see you so that I can hear from you exactly what it was you had in mind and so that any doubts that there may be between us can be resolved.

Yours sincerely

4.2 Performance

Both employer and employee have their respective duties to perform their part of the bargain made in the contract of employment. The employer will require the employee to give a fair day's work for a fair day's pay. At the commencement of the employment the employer will not know the full capabilities of the employee. For this reason many appointments are made on the basis of a probationary period of service as a 'getting to know you' element. This not only serves as an indication of the employee's potential in the performance of the tasks that are involved, but will give both parties an opportunity to establish whether or not the job is too demanding or that there is some incompatibility between them. If there is to be a period of probation this should be clearly understood from the outset and expressed in the letter of engagement. A paragraph of the nature of Letter 27 should be included.

Letter 27

Making a probationary contract

Dear

So that we may both have an opportunity to consider whether the job will be suitable for you, this engagement will be on a three month probationary basis. That means that at the end of three months you can decide, if you so wish, to leave us and we can decide, if we so wish, to end the employment. If at the end of this time we both agree that you should continue, then the employment will be confirmed on a permanent basis.

Yours sincerely

If at the end of the probationary period the appointment is confirmed then Letter 28 should be written.

Letter 28

Letter confirming appointment after probationary period

Dear

I am happy to be able to confirm that I am completely satisfied with the way in which you have carried out your duties during the past three months. I am pleased to be able to welcome you to the permanent staff and hope that your time with us will be long and successful.

Your sincererly

4.3 Obeying orders

The carrying out of any task for the employer requires that instructions should be given as to the performance of the task concerned. During the working day the employee will probably receive various orders and instructions and provided these are lawful and within the employee's compass, then the employee is required to obey them. Failure to do so will result in the employee being in breach of his or her contract of employment, and would entitle the employer to invoke the disciplinary procedures. During the probationary period the employer would be expected to make allowances as to performance, but not, of course, for refusal to carry out a lawful order.

The employee who is engaged as a general worker employed to perform unskilled tasks, will receive many orders during the day which he or she will be expected to perform without question. On the other hand, the skilled worker or one with particular talents and skills will be expected to perform the orders connected with the allotted tasks and to question orders or instructions that his or her experience and skill lead him/her to query. In any case of an order that may be open to question, the well-ordered organisation will have provided a grievance procedure for a disaffected employee and will entitle him or her to a hearing concerning orders which are considered to be unlawful or involve what could be considered a breach of the contract of employment. An example of what might be construed as an unlawful order which the employee could refuse to obey would be to perform a different task from that for which he or she was engaged. Letter 12 gives an example of the sort of circumstance where such an order might be given and refused. In the case envisaged by Letter 12 the consequence would be 'lay off'. A different circumstance would arise where the employer required the employee to move to another location within the organisation — although the contract of employment is silent upon the matter of mobility between locations. Unless the employee is willing to move as requested, then, in the absence of any provision in the contract that either expressly or by implication requires mobility, then the employee could refuse to comply with the order and should the employer then decide to take disciplinary action a complaint to the tribunal of 'unfair dismissal' could result. It is important for the employer to bear this

risk in mind whenever the question of discipline for refusal to
obey an order arises. An employee employed under a letter such
as Letter 2 can claim that his or her employment is at a fixed
workplace. To ask an employee to move means a change in the
contract terms for which he or she could reasonably ask to be
compensated. If the employee does agree to a change in workplace the change should be recorded as in Letter 29.

Letter 29

Letter confirming change of workplace

Dear

Thank you for your agreement to transfer from the filling station at
Main Road, Newtown, to the station at Planters Road. From time to
time it does become necessary for our Managers to move to new
sites and we are appreciative of your co-operation.

As agreed, I confirm that we will meet the extra travelling
expenses (£5 per week) that you will incur because of this change.

Yours sincerely

Where there is, in the employer's view, an unlawful refusal to
obey an order, then the disciplinary code must be borne in mind.
If there is no code, then none the less, except in the most
exceptional case, a warning procedure must be followed before
any dismissal. Without the warnings the risk of an unfair
dismissal claim exists with consequent penalty being imposed
upon the employer. Letters 24 and 25 are examples of warning
letters for breach of the contractual obligation to attend work at
the appropriate time. Letter 30 is a warning concerning disobedi-
ence to an order. Where health and safety is concerned, instant
dismissal could be justified, but again, to protect against subsequent claim, a letter such as Letter 30 should be written.

Letter 30

Letter giving warning for disobedience to a lawful order

Dear

You were told by Mr Jones to stop smoking whilst working at your machine. You are aware of the Company's rules on smoking and that it is not permitted except during the lawful tea break and then only in those areas set aside for smokers. These rules are made for good reason and must be obeyed. If you disobey the instructions given to you on this or any other lawful matter, you will be liable to dismissal. This letter is a formal warning and will be recorded on your record. If you consider that there is anything unfair, either in the order given to you by Mr Jones or in this letter, you have the right to express your point of view and appeal under the provisions of the code.

Yours sincerely

There are going to be occasions when the offence is so gross that instant dismissal is called for. The days when an employer could merely shout out 'you're fired' have gone. On instant dismissal an application by the employee to an industrial tribunal is a very high possibility. The question before the tribunal will be whether or not such strong action was justified. The employer must prepare to meet the challenge and should record as quickly as possible the reason for the action taken. Letter 31 should be written.

Letter 31

Letter confirming instant dismissal for breach of safety rules

Dear

This letter is to confirm, formally, the reason for your instant dismissal today.

All employees are aware that smoking is strictly forbidden in the spirit store. Notices are prominently displayed in the store as well as around the works. Despite this you were found in the store with a lighted cigarette in your mouth.

Such irresponsible conduct could result in a fire or, even worse, a violent explosion. The code of discipline makes it quite clear that anyone found smoking in the spirit store will be instantly dismissed and you have been treated accordingly.

Yours sincerely

Where health and safety is concerned, an employee is under a statutory duty, in addition to the common law duty, to exercise skills possessed to the best of his or her ability. This will be dealt with at greater length in the next chapter. This duty of care includes the operation of the plant and machinery in a safe and proper manner and in particular not to remove guards when operating machinery whether or not that is done to improve production or facilitate the employee's ability to operate the machine. This duty of care can be included in the disciplinary rules as a serious breach of contract which might lead to dismissal, both under the organisation's disciplinary rules and as a result of the employee's breach of the Health and Safety at Work Act. An employer must not turn 'a blind eye' to any practice which might result in injury or danger. It is also a wise precaution that any breach of this nature, even if no injury resulted, be recorded. If an injury results at any time, quite apart from any questions of employment law, claims for damages for personal injury will inevitably result. The employer's attitude to these practices will come into question. Any laxity by the employer is likely to be construed as acquiescence in the wrongdoing and defeat any defence that the employer may wish to raise that the employee was, in whole or in part, the author of his or her own misfortune. Not only should a warning letter be written whenever the wrong practice is observed, but a reminder notice should be circulated to all the relevant workforce. Letter 32 is a warning; Letter 33 is a reminder notice.

Letter 32

Warning letter for unsafe working practice

Dear

It has been reported to me that this morning your machine was seen running but with the guard removed. This is not only a clear breach of the working rules of the shop but also a serious danger to you and anyone else near to the machine.

You are formally being warned that the machine may not be started up unless the guard is in position and the guard may at no time be removed whilst the machine is working, whether that be for clearing obstructions or for facilitating the work being done. Repetition of this conduct can result in your dismissal.

Your sincerely

Letter 33

Notice reminding employees not to interfere with safety guards

All employees are reminded that it is a serious breach of the company's safety rules to interfere with the safety guards on the machines. These guards are there for the protection of the person using the machine. It will be considered a serious breach of the code of practice and an act of gross misconduct if anyone is found working with a machine whilst the guard is not properly in place. All employees are reminded that an act of gross misconduct can result in instant dismissal.

4.4 Trust and confidentiality

Matters concerning trust and confidentiality form an important part of the employee's contractual duty of faithful service. In some markets the confidentiality of the process: the market that the organisation seeks to supply; the patents that the organisation might have; customer lists; and trade contacts that are vital to the organisation's survival in the market place are matters that the employee is bound to keep secret not only during the employment, but also after the employment has ended. Document 2 includes a formal provision referring to this obligation. Even without an express clause in the contract the obligation exists. A formal contract of employment, such as is contained in Document 2, will contain a clause obliging the employee to give up any documents, notes or records in his or her possession when he or she leaves the employment. A distinction has to be drawn between trade secrets to which the employee has had access and information that the employee has gained as part of his or her skill. As an example, an employee may receive training in computer programming enabling him or her to write programs to suit a particular industry. The knowledge of programming that has been obtained is part of the employee's skill that he/she is entitled to use wherever he/she may work. If, however, during the course of the employment the employer has devised a specific programme to perform a particular service for the employer, that programme is part of the employer's trade secrets and may not be disclosed to a new employer. Where it is found that an ex-employee is breaking the obligation of confidentiality, then an action can be taken in the Courts for an injunction to restrain him or her. It is essential that action be taken quickly. Letter 34 could be written to an ex-employee in breach of the duty of confidentiality.

Letter 34

To ex-employee who is using confidential information

Dear

We have discovered that you are using our customer and pricing list to call on customers and solicit orders from them.

Unless you (a) return to us immediately all copies that you have of our customer and pricing lists and all other papers and documents in your possession relating to our business and (b) give us your undertaking that you will not in future make use of the knowledge that you have of our customers and pricing, we shall make an immediate application to the Court and in those proceedings we shall claim an injunction, damages and costs.

Please let us hear from you.

Yours sincerely

4.5 Gifts, tips and bribes

There are situations where the employer will allow certain gifts and small rewards from customers or clients in respect of the employee's services to those customers or clients. This is acceptable in some organisations; indeed in the catering industry, tips form a large part of the employee's remuneration. The bar employee being offered 'one for yourself', the delivery person being given a tip for prompt delivery and the waiter being given a 'present' for ensuring that the table required for the group is reserved are typical of the acceptable and normal course of events. There is, though, a dividing line between such small tokens of appreciation to a relatively humble employee and the more significant gifts given to an employee who is in a position to confer a valuable privilege on someone doing business with the employer. The buyer, for example, who is given a bottle of Scotch whisky at Christmas might be regarded as on the borderline. Where it was a holiday in Spain that was given, the borderline would clearly have been crossed. The question is asked, where is the dividing line between a present and a bribe? In those cases where the employee could be exposed to temptation the employer should lay down rules as to what is or is not acceptable. Letter 35 is a memorandum that could be sent to all those who might find themselves faced with possible temptation.

Letter 35

Memorandum as to gifts

For the guidence of all employees the following are the Company's rules relating to presents or rewards that may be offered by suppliers and others seeking to do business with the Company.

1. Unless offence will be caused, no employee should accept any gift, tip, entertainment or other reward from anyone who is doing business with the Company or who is hoping to do business with us.
2. No gift of money can at any time be accepted.
3. No gift having a significant value can be accepted. A gift worth more than £10 will be considered to have a significant value.
4. No entertainment, other than a normal working lunch or normal entertainment at a public house or bar can be accepted without previous permission.
5. Anyone who is offered a gift or entertainment which has to be refused because of these rules must report the offer and the circumstances in which it was made.
6. A breach of these rules will be considered a serious breach of contract by the employee and could lead to dismissal.

4.6 'Moonlighting'

The same question of 'faithful service' arises where an employee who has worked his or her daily hours for one employer then works for another after normal hours have been completed. Commonly known as 'moonlighting', and a part of modern employment in many industries, depending upon the terms of the contract of employment, there is nothing in law that would prevent an employee taking part-time work with another employer after his or her duties to the primary employer have been performed. Clause 3(c) of Document 2 imposes upon the employee the duty to devote 'his or her whole time and attention' to the employment. Where such a provision is included, work for another employer, or even self-employment, would be a breach of the contract. Such a provision would normally be included in a formal contract but would be very unusual in the oral or informal letter of appointment. In those cases the employee must not in taking extra work act contrary to the interests of his/her primary employer. The employee must ensure that his/her ability to perform duties to the primary employer is not in any way impaired. Any employee who carries out any work for a competitor should be considered a potential risk to the organisation. When the fact is discovered, assuming that there is nothing in the contract of employment that forbids such activity, the position of the other employer must be considered. If the employee is under contract and is then discovered to be doing work for another, especially if this is being done in the primary employer's time or with the primary employer's plant, not only is the employee liable to claim being made upon him/her for breach of contract, but also the competitor is liable for inducing that breach. There are rare examples of contracting out of employees who have a particular skill, but these cases are quite different. Where the situation is discovered, the primary employer must take action. The moonlighting employee must be warned that he/she has a duty to ensure that his or her health or ability to do the work, are not impaired, and if the employee is breaking the contract, the other employer must be warned of the consequences of continuing to encourage this wrongful action. Letter 36 could be written to the employee (again the point must be emphasised that these things are best recorded in writing; that way there is positive evidence which can be produced if any sort of legal proceedings come about) and Letter 37 to the other employer. Letter 36 has to be framed with care. It would be easy to write a letter containing an innuendo that the employee could claim was defamatory.

Letter 36

Letter to an employee who is moonlighting

Dear

It has come to my notice that after you finish work here, on most nights and at some weekends, you work part time for Smith & Co. Ltd.

What you do in your own time is, of course, a matter for you but I must urge you to consider your health and caution you against doing too much. Your work here must not be allowed to suffer, which must mean that you must get an adequate amount of rest.

I must also warn you that in some cases we are in direct competition with Smith & Co. Ltd and you must ensure that you do not disclose to them anything that you may have learned of our business, nor do anything that might help them in competition with us.

Yours sincerely

Letter 37

Letter to a rival employer regarding an employee who is in breach of contract

Dear Sir

We have learned that you are using the services of our Mr R. Jones to carry out drawing office work for you. We have discovered this because Jones has been found working on drawings for you in our drawing office, using our materials and in the time that he should have been performing his work for us.

We assume that you were not aware of these facts and we hope that now that you have been made aware of them you will ensure that there will be no repetition. Jones has been reprimanded. His employment with us would not prevent his working for you with his own materials and equipment and in his own time. Please ensure that, if you intend to ask him to give you further help, he is enabled to give that help without breaking his obligation to us.

Yours faithfully

4.7 Competition

So long as the contract of employment exists, the duty of fidelity means that the employee must not engage in any activity that brings him/her into competition with the employer. That duty, unless there is an express provision in the contract of employment such as clause 12 of Document 2, does not continue after the employment ends. Without a restriction of that nature the employee is free to engage in open competition with the former employer. A restriction on an employee must, though, stand the test of reasonableness. The general rule is that all clauses of that nature are considered to be 'in restraint of trade' and in principle are void. However, over the years the Courts have allowed clauses to be enforced that can be regarded as reasonable to protect the former employer's interests. To do otherwise would permit an employee effectively to steal away the employer's business. The test is whether the Court considers the clause to go beyond that which is fair to give the former employer protection; if the provisions exceed that which is necessary, then they are against the public interest and void. So long as the clause (technically described as a 'restrictive covenant') does not go against the public interest and is a reasonable restriction imposed upon the ex-employee or group of employees, then the Court will enforce the covenant and grant an injunction to prevent the ex-employee competing unfairly with the former employer. As an example, consider the hairdresser in the high street who has trained an employee to a high standard. The employee has, through the work, become known to the customers and has been able to impress them with his or her ability. If then the employee were to be allowed to leave and immediately open a salon next door, or even in the same town, the customers of the former employer could be attracted away. A restrictive covenant preventing this would in all probability be enforced. If the employee left and waited several years before setting up in competition, or if the new salon was opened up in a town many

miles away, the threat to the former employer would not be so
obvious and the clause might well be declared unenforceable in
that instance. In short, the Court will consider the length of time
that the restriction is to remain in force and the area over which
it is to operate. The Court would take into account the nature of
the enterprise that the employee had left, the sensitivity
of the employee's job, the employee's knowledge of the employer's
business, the particular skills of the employee and the size of the
market in which the business operates. A restriction worldwide
in extent, or imposing a lifelong obligation would rarely if ever
be supported. Only in cases which would concern the security of
the nation or the preservation of governmental secrets could such
a restriction be supported. In one celebrated decision, an inven-
tor of machine guns with a worldwide reputation in the field of
armaments was injuncted from worldwide competition. Where
an ex-employee is believed to be in breach of a restrictive
covenant, time is of the essence. It is not the sort of case where a
prudent business person would attempt to take action without
legal advice. A warning letter should be written and solicitors
consulted urgently. Letter 38 is the sort of letter to write.

Letter 38

To ex-employee in breach of covenant against competition

Dear

It has come to our notice that in breach of your agreement with us,
you are calling on customers in Newtown. We remind you of clause
12 of the agreement that you signed when you joined our organisation. That provided that you would not for a period of three years
from the end of your employment with us engage directly or
indirectly in any business competing with us within an area of
twenty-five miles from our office. You are breaking this agreement.

Unless we have your written undertaking by twelve noon on

Wednesday, that you will abide by the terms of your agreement (and we remind you that this term of the agreement is still effective even though you have left our employ) and will stop all attempts to sell to customers in this area, we shall instruct our solicitors to commence proceedings against you. In those proceedings we shall claim an injunction, damages and costs.

Yours sincerely

4.8 Interfering with suppliers and inducing a breach of contract

Interfering with suppliers or purchasers or procuring a breach of contract is another matter where a former employee may offend. The case here differs from that of unfair competition in that even though there may be no formal provision in the contract of employment the law will provide a remedy where the conduct complained of amounts to an attempt to persuade someone to break a contract. A formal contract of employment will usually contain a restriction against such behaviour. It often happens that an employee is induced to leave to join a rival organisation. There is nothing to prevent this unless the employee has been compelled to break his or her contract in order to take up the new position. Claim can, or course, be made against the employee but claim should also be made on the rival. Letter 39 is the sort of letter to write. Again this is no area of law for the layman. Legal advice should be sought. However, since it is important to move quickly a warning letter should be written. In the first paragraph, where the charge is being made that there is an inducement to break a contract, spell out concisely just what the contract was that was broken and give an indication of the reason for the belief that action was taken by the other party to induce the breach.

Letter 39

Letter of claim for inducing a breach of an employment contract

Dear Sir

In breach of his contract to be employed by us for a period of three years from 1 January 1990, John Smith has left us and has joined the organisation that you have established. From information that has reached us we have satisfied ourselves that it was at your instigation and with your encouragement and support that he has taken this action. We have suffered damage from this breach of contract and we are immediately instructing our solicitors to take proceedings against you.

Yours faithfully

It was this legal principle (what lawyers call the tort of inducing breach of contract) that in the early days of trade unionism was used to prevent unions calling workers out on strike. The law said that such activity amounted to an inducement by the union to the employees to break their contract to perform their duties to their employer. Because of this liability, Parliament passed legislation at the beginning of the century giving immunity to trade unions in such cases. The trade unions' position will be discussed in more detail in Chapter 9, but modern legislation has now changed the law and has removed some of the immunity against claims that the unions previously enjoyed. The term 'secondary action', which in effect means an interference with the employer's business when that employer is not the main employer in dispute with the trade union concerned, is now a civil offence. It is a matter that has concerned the Courts greatly over the past decade. The injured employer must apply to the court for an injunction (interdict in Scotland) and, if the injunction is disregarded, can obtain a measure of pressure upon the union by the sequestration of its assets (sequestration means that the assets are taken away and placed in the hands of someone else who keeps them and all income arising from them until such time as the offender abides by the order of the Court). Do not attempt to write any letters or take any action without first taking urgent legal advice.

4.9 Trade union membership

One other area of difficulty related to the concept of 'faithful service' and the performance of duties associated with employment arises when membership of a trade union is considered. The current legislation makes it lawful for any worker to join and be a member of a trade union, except only for work that is classified as inappropriate for union involvement such as at the government intelligence centre, GCHQ. The employer is not obligated to recognise a particular trade union associated with the particular industry but may not prevent any worker from joining a union. To dismiss an employee for joining or belonging to a union might result in a finding of 'unfair dismissal'. To recognise a trade union to which employees may belong is a matter for the employer. The employer might agree to pay the rate for the job that the union has negotiated or, indeed, he or she might pay above that rate. It is entirely a matter for the discretion of the employer. If, however, it is decided to recognise a particular trade union, an agreement will be entered into with the union. A specimen recognition agreement is given in Appendix B.

When an organisation contains a workforce who in part or in total are members of a recognised trade union that has negotiated the right to recruit members and to allow shop stewards and safety representatives to be elected and appointed to look after those members' interests, then the employee/union member has divided loyalties. He or she has a primary loyalty to the employer and a secondary loyalty to the union. Ideally, the contract of employment should state these loyalties clearly and should make clear that the primary duty of loyalty is to the employer. It should also be made clear by the employer that it is accepted that the employee/member will obey the rules and democratic processes of the union. When the agreement is first reached with a trade union that it will have the right to recruit amongst the workforce, a notice should be given to all employees. The notice will make clear the right of the employee to join, or refrain from joining the union. It will also set out the principles indicated above. Letter 40 is the type of notice to be given. Since at this stage of the relationship between union and employer, no one would wish to create a disharmony, it might be tactful to discuss the form of this notice with the union representative before circulating it.

Letter 40

Notice of trade union rights to recruit

JOHNSON CONGLOMERATES PLC

The Group have agreed with the General Workers' Union that it shall have the right to recruit members amongst the workforce of every Company in the Group. That union will be recognised as having the right to negotiate pay and conditions of work for its members and to have shop stewards and safety representatives elected by its members in the Group Companies. In reaching this agreement with the union the Company wishes to make two matters clear. Firstly, it recognises that there will be a duty of loyalty from the members to the union and that duty will expect members to observe the rules and democratic processes of the union. Secondly, the membership of the union does not override the duty of loyalty that is owed by every employee to the Company. Where those duties conflict, then the primary duty is to the Company upon whose existence and prosperity we all depend for our living.

4.10 Conflict of duties

Trade union safety representatives can find themselves in direct conflict with the employer in respect of their duties of loyalty and confidentiality. The elected and appointed safety representatives in an organisation that negotiates with a recognised trade union might have to investigate a serious or fatal accident at work. There is then a conflict of duties which representatives have to face. They have the statutory right to investigate the circumstances of the accident for and on behalf of the injured employee or his/her family and for the membership of the union and to make a report on their findings. The investigation might well lead the safety representative to the conclusion that the employer was wholly or partly to blame for the accident. The report submitted will be of some value as evidence in any legal proceedings. This will produce the conflict between the representative and his/her employers. The duty in this respect is to report fairly and without bias. If that duty is discharged faithfully, the representative must state honestly what he or she has found, even though that finding is against the interest of the employer. An exchange of letters in the form of Letters 41 and 42 might be helpful in reducing any possible misunderstandings as to the position faced by the representative.

Letter 41

Letter from safety representative to employer

Dear

Accident on 5 October

I am writing to you before making my report on this accident. I do recognise that I am an employee of the Company and I accept the duties that that employment creates. However, I am under an obligation to both the family of John Smith and to my union to report the relevant facts of matters which have led to this tragedy and my own conclusions based upon those facts.

I do not want you to think that I have wavered in my loyalty to the Company but I must carry out my duty faithfully. I do not want you to think that I am prejudging the issue – I have yet to complete my investigation. It may be that my conclusions are unfavourable to the Company. I have to make it clear that favourable or unfavourable, I must make my report and this I will do and I will give my views honestly and without fear or favour.

Yours sincerely

Letter 42

Letter from the Company to the safety representative

Dear

Thank you for your letter and for setting out your position so clearly. I am confident that you will report honestly and fairly and I can assure you that no obstacles will be put in your way.

Yours sincerely

CHAPTER 5

Health and safety at work

5.1 Historical background

One of the most significant and important Acts of Parliament that relate to employment within the United Kingdom is the Health and Safety at Work Act 1974. As long ago as 1833 concern was shown by enlightened industrialists as to the safety and welfare of employees working in manufacturing industries. This concern led to the passing of the Factory Acts of the nineteenth century which were designed to protect the very young and women who were employed in the heaviest industries of those times. The first generalised Act offering a degree of safety to all who were employed in manufacturing processes was passed in 1901 and began the legislative process that culminated in the Mines and Quarries Act 1954, the Factory Act 1961, and the Offices, Shops and Railway Premises Act 1963.

These Acts did not extend cover to all workers; for example, many places that operated plant were not classified as factories under the legislation and educational establishments and hospitals were not within the Offices, Shops and Railway Premises Act. All areas of work that were not specifically covered by the statutory provisions had no legal obligation as to health and safety. Common law duty rested upon the employer to provide a safe system of working and this duty must be insured in accordance with the provisions of the Employer's Liability (Compulsory Insurance) Act 1969. An employer who does not take out insurance to protect his/her employees under this Act is committing a criminal offence. When insurance is effected (and it has to be renewed every year), the insurance company will issue a certificate, much like the certificate of insurance that is issued to all motorists in respect of their cars. This certificate must be

77

displayed in a position where every person employed can see and read it without difficulty.

The 1974 Act has now covered all the areas that were previously not covered by legislation. The Act and the regulations that have been made under it impose upon employers duties to secure so far as is reasonably practicable the health, safety and welfare of all employees. These duties are enforced by an inspectorate which has powers of entry upon the business premises to satisfy itself that the statutory duties are being performed. Criminal liability rests upon the employer who is in breach. This liability can result in imprisonment of an offender. More than this, breach can result in an employee claiming that it amounts to a fundamental breach of contract of employment, entitling the employee to resign and claim that he or she was constructively dismissed.

5.2 Safety policy

One of the duties that the Act imposes is that every company having more than five employees has to prepare and, as necessary, revise, a written statement of the general policy with respect to the health and safety at work of the employees. This statement must be displayed prominently. The document should state, in broad terms, the management's intent and commitment to the health and safety of employees. It should include reference to the general responsibilities of all within the organisation, and who is responsible for the monitoring and imposition of the policy, and indicate to all employees that a duty and legal obligation lies upon them to take care of their own and others' health and safety. The policy must be dated and regularly revised according to the changing conditions in the workplace. It should indentify areas of particular hazard that might exist and specify the safe system of work that is expected to be operated. The statement should be written in plain terms so that all can understand it, and the attention of all employees must be drawn to it. Document 4 is a specimen of a simple statement of safety policy.

Document 5

Statement of safety policy

The health and safety policy of this Company (pursuant to the Health and Safety at Work Act 1974)

Dated 21 January 1991

1. It is the policy of this Company to provide healthy and safe working conditions for all employees. The Company recognises and accepts its responsibilities in connection with the provision of adequate safety measures and the prevention of accidents.

2. This Company will not allow any unsafe working practices to operate in any department and it is the responsibility of the individual manager of each department to ensure that the welfare and safety of all the employees under his or her supervision at all times takes precedence over any other consideration. In the event of any problems arising out of this responsibility, it is the duty of the manager to raise the matter with the appropriate director of the Company and, in the last resort, with the mangaging director.

3. The following will be among the priorities of the management:

    (a) to ensure that plant, equipment and systems of work are safe.

    (b) to make safe arrangements for the use, handling, storage and transport of articles and substances used within the premises or any process carried on as part of the business of the Company.

    (c) to ensure that there is sufficient information, instruction, training and supervision to enable all employees to avoid hazards and contribute positvely to their own safety and health at work.

    (d) to ensure that employees have a safe place of work and safe access to it.

    (e) to provide a safe working environment.

    (f) to provide adequate welfare facilities.

4. It is recognised that the safety policy is only likely to be effective if it is supported by the active co-operation of all employees. In

this respect, employees are reminded of their own obligations under the Act. The Act provides that every employee, whilst at work, has the duty:

(a) to take reasonable care for the health and safety of him-herself and of other persons who may be affected by his/her acts or omissions at work; and

(b) to co-operate with his or her employer, or any other person, in ensuring that requirements or duties imposed by the relevant statutory provisions are complied with; and

(c) not intentionally or recklessly to interfere with or misuse anything provided in the interests of health, safety or welfare in pursuance of the statutory provisions.

If any employee fails to observe these basic principles he or she will face disciplinary action that could result in dismissal.

5. All injuries, however slight, must be reported to the employee's supervisor or manager and must be entered in the accident book as reported. The accident book is situated in   .

6. First aid boxes are situated at   .

7. Any person discovering a fire shall contact   . If it is possible for that person to extinguish the fire without danger to him- or herself then he or she shall immediately do so, otherwise immediate evacuation of the building must take place following the fire drill as laid down and practised. Fire extinguishers are placed at   .

8. The Company's fire procedure is displayed on the notice board in   and all heads of department are aware of the procedure to be followed in the event of any emergency. It is the responsibility of everyone to ensure that all fire doors are kept closed, unlocked and clear and free from obstruction.

9. The person with the overall responsibility for the implementation of this policy is   .

THIS STATEMENT OF POLICY WILL BE REVIEWED, ADDED TO OR MODIFIED FROM TIME TO TIME AND MAY BE SUPPLE-MENTED IN APPROPRIATE CASES BY FURTHER STATEMENTS RELATING TO THE WORK OF THE PARTICULAR DEPART-MENTS OR PARTICULAR GROUPS OF EMPLOYEES.

Signed

Managing Director

It is the responsibility of the employer not only to prepare and display a statement of safety policy but also to ensure that the policy is specifically drawn to the attention of employees. An opportunity should be taken to include with the wages packet a note drawing attention to the policy. It would be a useful opportunity, when sending this note, to make specific reference to the employee's obligations with an example of the way that these obligations arise. Letter 43 could be such a note. Every time the safety policy is revised a fresh note should be sent, and there is no harm in repeating the examples of employee responsibilities. Each new employee should have a copy of this note in his or her first wages packet.

Letter 43

Note of statement of safety policy

The attention of all employees is drawn to the statement of the Company's health and safety policy which is displayed on the notice board in   .

Your attention is particularly drawn to your own duties. You have a duty to have regard to your own safety. This means, amongst other things, that where safety clothing has to be worn it is the duty of foremen and others to ensure that the clothing is available. IT IS ALSO THE DUTY OF THE EMPLOYEES TO WEAR THE CLOTHING AT ALL TIMES THAT THEY ARE ENGAGED UPON WORK FOR WHICH THAT CLOTHING HAS BEEN DESIGNED. ANY EMPLOYEE WHO DISREGARDS THIS DUTY WILL BE LIABLE TO DISCIPLINARY ACTION WHICH COULD INCLUDE DISMISSAL.

You will also see that employees may not interfere with anything that is provided by the Company pursuant to the obligations imposed upon it by the Health and Safety at Work Act 1974. THE REMOVAL OF SAFETY GUARDS FROM MACHINES IS AN OFFENCE FOR WHICH NOT ONLY WILL THE EMPLOYEE BE LIABLE TO DISMISSAL, BUT ALSO IS A CRIMINAL OFFENCE, FOR WHICH HE OR SHE MAY BE CHARGED IN THE MAGISTRATES' COURT AND FINED.

5.3 Occupier's liability

Quite apart from an employer's duties under the Health and Safety at Work Act, every occupier of property has a duty to protect all who come onto the premises from harm due to any defect upon the premises. This would mean, for example, that there is a duty to protect workers sent by another employer to decorate the premises. If there is some inherent danger, for example an uneven floor, then some warning must be given of the fact. A verbal warning carries with it the danger that it is not heard or understood, and even more it raises the problem that in the event of an accident it is difficult (in the case of a fatal accident perhaps impossible) to prove that the warning was ever given. Whilst the display of warning notices, wherever possible, is obviously a necessity, where they cannot be displayed or where they are obviously being ignored, both for self-protection and to protect the position of insurance, some written record of the warning should be given. Letter 44 is an example.

Letter 44

Letter recording warning of dangerous premises

The Managing Director
Factory Decorating Services Ltd
9 John Street
Newtown

Dear Sir

Your workmen are on these premises carrying out the works of decoration in accordance with your contract with us.

I must draw your attention to the fact that I have on two occasions now warned the foreman in charge and the painter concerned of the danger in using unsupported ladders on the floor of the paint shop here. The floor of the shop is stained with paint residues and is for that reason slippery; it is also uneven. There are warning notices displayed drawing attention to this fact and all who use the shop are urged to take especial care. Despite this, your painters are using ladders which are unsupported in any way.

The responsibility for the safe working of your employees rests upon you. I would have thought that the only safe way in which the upper parts of the shop could be reached is by the use of a scaffold tower. The shop has been cleared of all plant to allow free access for your men and there is adequate room for the use of scaffold.

Yours faithfully

5.4 Common law duties

Even before there were any statutory duties laid upon employers, the common law placed upon everyone the duty to take care and to see that no injury was caused to third parties from the activities that were being undertaken. This duty was gradually extended into the area of law that lawyers called 'the law of master and servant'. It became established under the principles of that branch of the law that an employer was liable for negligence if an employee became injured because of something that the employer should have foreseen. If, therefore, it can be foreseen that there might be a danger, employees must be warned and an attempt made to protect them against the danger. It is also a legal principle (which lawyers always express in the Latin words *volenti non fit injuria*) that you cannot complain if you are injured through some risk that you voluntarily accepted. In Letter 43, in capital letters, the employees' attention was drawn to the fact that they must wear protective clothing where it has been provided for them. If an employee is injured through failure to carry out instructions to wear a hard hat in a hard hat area, the defence of *volenti* could be raised. The difficulty with this defence is that to be totally successful, the employer would have to show that the employee was entirely responsible for his or her injuries. If there is only 1 per cent blame on the employer, he or she can be made liable. The damages are assessed and then apportioned between the employee and employer in the proportions to which they were to blame. The employer must try to see that where there is a risk, not only does the employee know about it but that he or she accepts the risk to the total exclusion of the employer. This is a difficult thing to achieve. On the other hand, short of removing the risk entirely (and this is often just not possible) there is no way of preventing someone from doing something completely foolish. Removing the guards from a machine is a very common example. The display of a notice is not enough. Too often notices go unread. A written warning is essential and the pay packet is a most convenient means of delivery. Letter 43 is one attempt to bring home the message. Letter 44 is another. Where an employee has been seen breaking the safety rules, give a written warning. Chapter 6 discusses the question of written warnings before dismissing an employee. A letter of warning should be issued over breaches of safety rules. Letter 45 is such a letter.

Letter 45

Letter of warning of breach of safety rules

Dear

It has been reported to me that in direct breach of the safety rules, you were discovered to be operating your machine with the guard removed.

Notices forbidding this practice are displayed and your attention to the rules has been drawn by written notice with your wage packet. None the less you have removed the guard whilst the machine was in operation.

This conduct is a breach of the terms of your employment and justifies dismissal. On this occasion you are being warned. The Company expressly forbids this behaviour. We take every opportunity to prevent the removal of guards when the machines are operating but clearly it is not possible to maintain continuous observation of operatives whilst they are working. If you repeat this behaviour, you will be instantly dismissed. If through your irresponsible disregard of orders you suffer injury, it will be entirely your own fault and no liability for any injury will be accepted by the company.

Yours sincerely

5.5 Insurance

Every employer is under a legal duty to effect insurance against claims for damages in respect of injuries and death being brought by employees or their dependants. The insurance company issues the employer with a certificate of insurance which the employer is under a duty to display on the work premises. It is, it must be emphasised, a criminal offence not to effect such an insurance or to fail to display the certificate that evidences the cover. It is important for employees to realise that it is the employer who is covered by the policy, not the employee. So far as third parties are concerned, that is to say people who are not employees, they also have a right to claim for injuries that may suffer. Those injuries will normally be covered either by a separate occupiers' or public liability policy or by a separate section of a general policy taken out by the employer to cover him- or herself against all possible risks. It is important when making a proposal for any such policy that the insurance company is made aware of all matters which could conceivably be of significance to it when assessing the risk that it is being asked to undertake. If there are especially hazardous processes being carried out, or if dangerous products are being stored upon the premises, this must be disclosed. The record of past incidents, whether or not they involved an insurance claim, must be disclosed. Failure to do this can result in the insurers refusing to meet a claim. It is a great temptation to think that disclosure is going to increase the premiums. It may well do that, but that is a better business decision than to conceal relevant matters, pay premiums and find when the claim is made that failure to disclose has allowed the insurance company to refuse the claim. Letter 46 is the sort of letter to write when proposing for cover.

Letter 46

Letter with a proposal for insurance cover

Dear Sirs

I enclose a proposal form for employer's liability insurance and for occupier's liability insurance.

So far as concerns employer's liability, whilst we have never suffered any formal claim for injury suffered by any workman, it is right that you should know that one employee did suffer minor cuts when, in breach of all instructions, he removed the guard from a machine on which he was working. I enclose a copy of the letter that was written to him following that incident.

So far as concerns occupier's liability, the process carried on in these premises requires the use of methylated spirits which, under licence, are purchased and stored in an external fireproof store.

I await hearing from you with the quotation of the premium.

Yours faithfully

5.6 Dealing with injuries

When an incident occurs, write immediately to the insurance company, even if it is thought that either no claim will result or that any claim can be resisted. As in the case of a proposal, the insurers can refuse to meet a claim if their position has been compromised by something said (or not said) or done by the claimant. It may be that you are not sure whether or not the insurance policy covers the matter in question. None the less, the insurers should be notified. Leave it to them to say that the matter is not covered. Who knows, they may take the view that they are at risk and take over the claim, or it may be that when your lawyers look into the wording of the policy, they will advise that you have rights. Keep your options open. Above all, do not admit anything. More than that, do not think that because there is nothing in writing, what you say has no effect. Oral statements are as damaging as written ones. On becoming aware of an incident, check immediately that there is an entry in the accident book. Get statements from everyone remotely connected. Get them in writing and get them signed if you can. If you cannot persuade the witness to sign his or her statement, write it out yourself and add that the statement was taken down by you but that the witness refused to sign, then sign it yourself. Write down at the first opportunity what you saw and did. That statement will be available to you to refer to in any proceedings. The problem with all claims that end up in Court is the length of time it takes for a disputed matter to come to trial. Two or three years would be quick! Over that period of time memory fades. In law, the only documents that you are allowed to look at to refresh your memory are what are called 'contemporaneous notes'. That is, something that was written down at the first available opportunity. Document 6 is the sort of note that you would write down.

Document 6

Note of an incident

At 14.30 [it is well to use the twenty-four hour clock particularly when the works operate a twenty-four hour shift] on Wednesday 6 January 1991 I was in my office, which is at the north end of the machine shop on the ground floor of the works. [Say exactly where you were when you were first involved.] Joe Brown came running in and in an excited manner said that there had been an accident. He said that William Smith had been working on the small press making press-ings for the Thompson PLC order. He said that Smith had removed the guard from his machine so as to clear away a piece of metal that had broken off under the press. For some reason which he could not explain, the press had operated and Smith's hand had been crushed. [Most of this evidence is 'hearsay' but, none the less, record it]. I immediately went with Brown to the machine. Smith was in a state of shock. His hand was a bloody mess. Standing round him were John Taylor, who works the adjoining machine, Stan Green and Thomas Williams. Arthur Johnson, who is the company's first-aider, was attempting to staunch the flow of blood and to apply a dressing. The machine was switched off but the guard was re-moved. [Describe in as much detail as you can exactly what you saw and who was present.] I immediately ordered Taylor to rush to the telephone and call for an ambulance. Smith was conscious and I thought that it was safe for him to be moved. I therefore told Johnson to help me take him into my office. This we did. My secretary made a cup of tea which she gave Smith and he drank it. Johnson had managed to staunch the bleeding and had a dressing on the injury. Whilst we were waiting for the ambulance, I made an entry in the accident book and I telephoned the Health and Safety Officer reporting the incident and requesting report forms. The ambulance arrived at about 15.30 (I did not note the exact time) and

Smith was taken to hospital. I then called Brown in to my office and I took a statement from him on what he had seen and done. After Brown I called in Taylor, Williams and Johnson and took statements from them. Williams was reluctant to tell me anything and refused to sign what I had written down. I signed the statement I had written for him. Green had left the building. I had noticed when we were at the machine that he looked very white. When I asked for him to come to see me, I was told by Williams that Green had gone to the toilet, had been sick and had gone home. [Write down, with as much detail as you can, exactly what you did and what you observed of others. Do not try to be a lawyer. Record everything, even things that are going to be excluded as hearsay. Work on the principle that every piece of information is going to be needed by the lawyers – whether they use it as direct evidence or whether they use it in cross examination of witnesses is their task.]

Having dealt with the immediate crisis, now is the time to notify the insurers. It is as well that the company's lawyers are also alerted to a possible claim. There is no need to do more at this stage than warn them and see that they have copies of everything. Write Letter 47 to the insurers and Letter 48 to the lawyers.

Letter 47

Letter to insurers notifying a possible claim

Dear Sirs

Employer's liability insurance policy no. 1234567

We have to notify you of an incident that occurred today which may give rise to a potential claim under the above-mentioned policy.

    We enclose a statement made by our Works Manager Mr Stephen Duncan, together with other statements from other workmen which describe the incident. We also enclose a copy of the entry in the Company's accident book and a copy of the report made to the

Health and Safety Authority. Whilst no claim has yet been made, we must anticipate that in due course one will come. We have made no admissions of any liability. It is our view that the Company has no liability. It is and always has been our firm policy that no machine may be kept switched on whilst the guard is removed.

Will you please acknowledge this letter and confirm that you accept that any claim will be covered by the above policy.

Yours faithfully

Letter 48

Letter to lawyers following an accident

Dear

I confirm my telephone conversation [it is best that you speak to the lawyers at an early opportunity to explain what has happened and why you are going to send them material] of this morning when I told you of the unfortunate incident here yesterday.

I have notified our insurers, and I enclose for your records a copy of our insurance policy, a copy of the letter I wrote to the insurance company, a copy of the various statements I took, a copy of the entry in the accident book and a copy of the report that I have made to the Health and Safety Authority. To give you the whole picture, I also enclose a copy of the notice that was given to everyone in their wages packet. A notice of this sort would have been included in Smith's wages packet on 5 December last. [This is where Letter 43 becomes very relevant.]

As I told you, I do hope that we will not have to involve you and that the insurance company will accept the claim and protect our interests. You might, though, just look through what I have sent you and say whether there is anything else that you think I should do.

Yours sincerely

Any consultant advising a company on its health and safety obligations will give his or her client a formal set of advice notes laying out the principles of precautions and good practices to be followed. A specimen of such a brief is set out in Appendix C. In

the brief will be seen a section relating to records of accidents.
There are two different types of incident that require notification:
'Dangerous occurrences' (the brief sets out what these are), and
accidents which cause injury or death of an employee. Notification is to the inspector at the local authority. In the case of
dangerous occurrences notification has to be on a 'prescribed
form'. This means that the form must be obtained from the local
authority. In the case of an accident (basically any serious
accident involving a fracture of any bone or any serious cut) the
authority must be informed by the quickest possible means,
which probably means a telephone call. That report must be
followed up by a written report which again has to be on a form
provided by the authority. Where as a consequence of an injury
received at work an employee dies within one year of the
accident causing the injury, the employer has to inform the
authority in writing whether or not the original injury was
reported at the time. Letter 49 is appropriate in the case of a
'dangerous occurrence', Letter 50 in the case of an accident and
Letter 51 where notice is received of a death within twelve
months. It may be thought that, having telephoned, no further
letter is necessary. In law it may not be necessary but since it
can involve the company in criminal proceedings if notification is
not given, always record by a letter a telephone message of this
nature. You cannot rely upon the authority's clerk to make a
note that a call has been made.

Letter 49

Reporting a dangerous occurrence

The Health and Safety Officer
West Riding District Council

16 January 1991

Dear Sir

Dangerous occurrence at Newtown Works

I confirm my telephone call of this morning when I informed your

Mr   [always ask for the name of the individual to whom you are speaking] that there had been an explosion in our spirit store this morning.

Will you please let me have as a matter of urgency a copy of the prescribed form of report for completion and submission to you.

Yours faithfully

Letter 50

Reporting an accident

The Health and Safety Officer
West Riding District Council

16 January 1991

Dear Sir

I confirm my telephone conversation of this morning. I am unable to give the name of the individual with whom I spoke as he declined to give me his name.

There was a serious accident in our works this morning when an employee suffered a crushed hand in one of the presses. Will you please let me have as speedily as possible the appropriate form upon which I may make a formal report to your authority.

Yours faithfully

Letter 51

Reporting a death within twelve months

The Health and Safety Officer
West Riding District Council

16 January 1991

Dear Sir

re William Smith deceased

We have just been informed of the death of William Smith, a former employee residing at the time of his death at 6 Flower Lane, Newtown.

We are informed by the widow of the deceased that the cause of his death was stated to be related to the injury which he suffered at these works last June. We refer you to the report on that accident which we made to you on 21 June 1990.

This letter is written to you in discharge of our statutory obligations.

Yours faithfully

5.7 Powers of enforcing authorities

The Health and Safety at Work Act 1974 established a Health and Safety Commission and a Health and Safety Executive from whom help and advice can be obtained. The address is Health And Safety Commission (Inquiry Room), Baynards House, 1 Chepstow Place, London W2 4TF. They have the power to direct that an inquiry be held to report on any accident. District councils are created as the responsible authorities for enforcing the provisions of the Act and, in carrying out their duties, the authorities appoint inspectors with extensive powers of entry, inspection and interrogation. If following from the exercise of those powers an inspector considers that there is a continuing contravention of the obligations imposed under the Act, the inspector can serve an improvement notice requiring the contravention to be rectified within a specified period. If the inspector regards any contravention as involving a risk of serious injury, he or she can go further; a prohibition notice can be served. A prohibition notice takes effect immediately and the activity complained of must stop at once. In both cases there are rights of appeal. Where an improvement notice has been served, the inspector has the power to extend the time for compliance. If an improvement notice has been served, structural alteration of the premises may be needed, as where the matter complained of involves extra light or ventilation. The first action where the premises are held on lease in such a case would be to notify the landlord, Letter 52. Of course if the lease prohibits structural alteration and the landlord refuses consent, there is little that can be done to force the landlord's co-operation. In such a case the business faces the serious consequence that the activity must stop and new premises be found. For this reason, if for no other, before taking premises or embarking upon a new activity it is essential that the utmost consideration be given to the health and safety aspects of the work. It is also only prudent that before embarking upon work, the inspector is asked to say that the work will meet with the requirements of the notice (Letter 53).

Letter 52

Letter to landlord following an improvement notice

Dear

We have been served by the health and safety inspector with a notice complaining that there is inadequate ventilation in the paint shop and requiring the opening of an additional window or the installation of an air extraction ventilator in the south wall. Either solution will involve some interference with the structure of the wall.

Our surveyors advise that this can be done without weakening the structure and without causing any damage to the appearance of the property. We enclose a copy of the plans that they have prepared showing the work that is proposed.

May we please ask for your consent to this work being carried out. We accept that it will be done at our expense and that we will be liable for any costs or fees that you may incur.

We have been given two months by the inspector to comply with his notice and would therefore be grateful if you could help us by giving a speedy decision.

Yours faithfully

Letter 53

Letter to inspector asking for approval of proposed works

Dear

Following from your improvement notice, we enclose herewith plans showing the work which we propose to carry out in compliance.

Will you please confirm that if work is carried out in accordance with these plans, your notice will be satisfied.

Yours faithfully

Assuming that the landlord gives consent and the work is put in hand, there are clearly two possibilities: first that the work cannot be carried out within the time allowed, in which case an application has to be made for an extension (Letter 54); or the work is finished within the time, in which case the inspector must be notified and asked for his or her confirmation that there is no further problem (Letter 55).

Letter 54

Letter asking for an extension of improvement notice

Dear

The works required by your improvement notice have been put in hand. Unfortunately we were required under the terms of our lease to obtain the consent of our landlord. The necessary formalities involved in the grant of a licence from him caused considerable delay and the builders have only this week been able to commence work. They inform me that the work will take a further three weeks to complete.

Could you please take this letter as a formal application to extend the time for compliance with the notice by a period of one month.

Yours faithfully

Letter 55

Letter reporting compliance with improvement notice

Dear

We are pleased to inform you that we have completed the works necessary to comply with the improvement notice served by you and invite you to inspect the premises again.

Please confirm the time of your inspection so that we can arrange for our surveyor to be present to answer any questions. Following the inspection we trust that you will give formal confirmation that the notice has been complied with.

Yours faithfully

5.8 Trade union involvement

Where the employer and a trade union or unions are parties to an agreement as to the terms and conditions of the workplace, then the employer has legal obligations to the union and its officials, both full-time and the lay-elected shop stewards within the employer's own workforce. By regulations made under the Health and Safety at Work Act 1974 (the Safety Representatives Regulations 1978), the employer who recognises and negotiates with the relevant trade union has a duty to recognise and accept that the union has the right to elect and appoint a member of the employer's workforce as a safety representative. This shop-floor representative is somewhat different from the traditional shop steward, whose duties would be governed by the mandate of the members on normal matters of discipline and grievance before the employer. The safety representative is not under such a restraint but has the legal right to inspect the workplace and

the system of work being operated, and then make representa-
tions to the employer so far as potential hazard or unsafe
practice is concerned. In effect, the safety representative acts as a
'works monitor' of the employer's workplace.

The employer also has the legal duty to assist in the setting up
of safety committees if this is requested by the safety representative. These committees are equally representative of both the
workforce and the management. The company safety officer
would normally hold a watching brief at the meetings, which
would be chaired by someone from the management side who
has authority over the financial commitments of the company for
the health and safety of all within it.

Unlike the industrial shop steward, the safety representative
does not have the power to 'stop the job'. Only in situations
arising from the onset of a hazardous works practice, or an
accident that could be repeated, could the safety representative
call in the shop steward and, if there was a failure to agree with
the employer, the shop steward could call for cessation of work
pending a resolution of the dispute. Possibly for this reason, it is
the practice of some unions to procure that the shop steward and
the safety representative is one and same person.

When, following agreement with the union, a safety representative is appointed there should be an exchange of letters
between the union and the employer, confirming the position.
Letters 56 and 57 are the appropriate letters.

Letter 56

Letter to employer to recognise an elected safety representative

Dear

On behalf of the   union I have to inform you that John Brown,
one of our members in your workforce, has been elected and
appointed safety representative for the workforce at New Factory,
Newtown. As safety representative he is the representative for the
workforce and the union.

As no doubt you are aware, by virtue of the Safety Representatives and Safety Committees Regulations (SI500/78) there is an obligation on the employer to recognise and accept the duly appointed trade union safety representative as a trade union lay official.

I trust that you will accept John Brown as the accredited safety representative for the membership within your organisation and that you will co-operate with him and permit him time off for training in matters of health and safety at work. The time off will be in accordance with the negotiated terms and conditions as applicable to the shop stewards in your organisation and in line with the recommendations of the legislation.

Yours sincerely

Letter 57

Letter from the employer accepting the trade union's appointee

Dear

Thank you for your letter of 11 January 1991, which I have considered. I note that John Brown has been appointed safety representative for the works at New Factory and will act for and on behalf of the membership within my organisation at those works.

I will recognise Brown's trade union status under the legislation and trust that he will act within the spirit of the Regulations and co-operate with my Safety Officer in the continuance of the high standards of health and safety practised within this organisation.

I will further ensure that, where reasonably practicable, he will be granted time off to take any relevant courses that are applicable to health and safety at work.

Yours sincerely

CHAPTER 6

Termination of employment

6.1 Introduction

Prior to 1971 ordinary employees had no remedy if they were dismissed. If an employee had a contract for a fixed period, he/she had a claim for damages for breach of contract if dismissed before the end of that term. There was no concept of fairness in the ending of an employment. Registered dock workers were an exception to this rule; they could take their grievance to an appeals committee who would decide whether or not the employer had acted fairly.

The Industrial Relations Act 1971 changed the law. It created an Industrial Relations Court and industrial tribunals to whom an aggrieved employee could appeal if he or she considered the dismissal unfair. The tribunals and the Industrial Relations Court were established as an informal and simple forum intended to be free from legal formalities. They were modelled on the Dock Labour Board's scheme with a legally qualified chairperson aided by two lay members, one a representative of the trade union side and the other of the employer.

The great hopes that informality and simplicity would rule the proceedings have to a large extent not been achieved. The combination of statutory rules as to dismissal, and the growth of case precedents interpreting the law and the rules, has complicated the procedures and made the dismissal of an employee a matter of considerable risk for an employer. It is no longer the case that a dismissal will be judged purely on the merits of an employer's reasons for the dismissal.

6.2 Dismissal procedure

When an employee has to be dismissed, to ensure that he or she will have no reliable proposition to put forward alleging unfair dismissal, the employer must show that the matter has been dealt with under a fair and reasonable procedure. This will require the employer to follow certain basic rules as to warnings, both oral and written, before any action is taken to terminate the employment. The onus is on the employer to show, when defending a claim, that a dismissal was fair and that he or she has acted properly and fairly in the preceding steps that resulted in the action taken. Unless this evidence is available, then the employer will have difficulty in answering the claim. A decision of the House of Lords in 1988 (*Polkey* v. *A. E. Dayton Services Ltd*, 1987 1 IRLR 503) made it clear that no matter what was the reason for the dismissal, the employer must show that there has been a procedure that the employee can recognise as being applicable to him or her, and that the procedure allows for that employee to follow a reasonable path through internal appeals and proper investigation before the dismissal is effective.

6.3 Warning procedures

Faced with the fact that an employee has committed some act amounting to misconduct, the employer must react to this breach and take measures to deal with it. Unless the act was some serious act of gross misconduct demanding instant dismissal, the initial response will be a warning. Bearing in mind that in the event of a claim, the employer will have to prove his or her actions, some written evidence of the warning should be made. In the case of a minor matter, a verbal warning would suffice but the fact that a warning had been given should be entered on the employee's record and the employee told that this has been done. If the misconduct is repeated – for example bad time keeping – then the next step must be a first written warning. Letter 58 is an example.

Letter 58

First written warning

14 January 1991

John Green

You are well aware that as part of our special relationship with our clients, we place the utmost importance on time keeping. It is essential that you are at work by 9.30 a.m. to receive calls from clients, and that you do not leave before 5 p.m. unless you have been given permission.

You have been warned before of your bad time keeping, and you were told on the last occasion that the verbal warning you had been given had been noted on your personnel file. In spite of that warning your time keeping has not improved and on three days this week, without any justification, you have been over an hour late for work.

This is a formal letter of warning to you that you must be at your place of work strictly in accordance with the terms of your employment. If you do not improve your time keeping, further disciplinary action will be taken.

This warning is being recorded on your personnel file.

Yours sincerely

Personnel Manager

Should this warning be ignored then a second written warning must be given. Letter 59 is such a letter.

Letter 59

Second written warning

John Green

You were given a verbal warning about your bad time keeping and on 14 January last, a formal written warning was given to you for the same matter.

As your time keeping still fails to reach the standard that we require, in view of our obligations to our clients, and as in consequence you are still not observing your contractual obligations to the Company, we have no alternative but to issue this second formal warning. If you fail to take this warning seriously and make a serious improvement in your time keeping, a final written warning will be issued.

It is essential that all our employees are properly informed of their responsibilities. It was for this reason that you were given a written statement of the terms of your employment when you joined the Company. In those terms you will see, clearly set out, the hours of work and the action you can take if you feel that you have a grievance. All employees, having been informed of their responsibilities, are expected to observe the terms of their contract of employment. You are no exception to this rule.

If there is any particular matter that is causing you a problem and contributing to your bad time keeping, then you should see your departmental supervisor or, if you prefer, see me so that we can see if there is any way in which the Company can help you.

This warning is being recorded on your personnel file.

Yours sincerely

Personnel Manager

If despite these two warnings there is no improvement, before any dismissal it is necessary to give a final warning.

Letter 60

Final warning

John Green

You have ignored the two written warnings given to you. You have not given any explanation for your bad time keeping nor taken the opportunity offered to you to discuss any problems that you might have.

Your behaviour is not acceptable. We therefore give you this last and final warning, which as with the previous warnings is being entered on your personnel file. Unless your time keeping improves and you present yourself for work each working day at the hours stated in your contract of employment, you will be subject to dismissal.

You are reminded of your right of appeal against this warning. Any appeal may be made as stated in the statement of terms and conditions of employment given to you when you joined the Company. If you have mislaid your copy of these terms and conditions a further copy can be obtained from the pay office.

Yours sincerely

Personnel Officer

If this final warning is ignored, then the employer can exercise his or her contractual right to end the employment. The employee, in a case such as this where the offence is not a grave and serious misconduct, is entitled to receive notice of the ending of his or her employment. The contract of employment may say how much notice has to be given. For example, in Letter 2 the contract was said to be subject to four weeks' notice, whilst in Document 2 it was three months' notice. Whatever the contract says, the notice must not be shorter than the period specified in the Employment Protection (Consolidation) Act 1978 as amended. If the employee has been employed for less than two years, the minimum period is one week. If the employment is for more than two but less than twelve years, the period is one week for each year of service. Over twelve years, the period is twelve weeks. The notice should be given in writing and Letter 61 is the form.

Letter 61

Notice dismissing an employee

John Green

Despite a verbal warning and three written warnings, you have chosen to continue with your practice of coming to work late. In view of this blatant breach of the terms of your employment we hereby give you   weeks' notice to terminate your employment.

Yours sincerely

Personnel Manager

6.4 Statement of reasons

The employee is entitled to demand a written statement giving particulars of the reasons for dismissal and those reasons may be put in evidence in any proceedings for unfair dismissal. If he or she makes such a demand, the employer must give the required particulars within fourteen days of the request. In a case such as has been illustrated in the previous letters, it is unlikely that any such request would be made and, in any event, the notice itself explains the reasons. If a request were to be made in those circumstances, the reply would be obvious 'the reason for dismissal was bad time keeping'. Any statement given should be succinct and confined to a bald statement of the fact. In a case such as that in Letter 31, the reason would be 'in breach of safety rules the employee was found smoking in the spirit store'. In a case such as is exemplified in Letter 62 it would be 'the employee was found drunk in the driving seat of the Managing Director's car'. The employer must remember that the statement of reasons may be given in evidence and if too much is said, then the path is opened for the employee's lawyer to cross examine to establish that the reason given was not a true reason. There is no particular format for a statement of reasons but Document 7 could be followed.

Document 7

Employer's statement of reasons for dismissal

John Green

In response to your request dated 14 January 1991 and received by us on 16 January 1991 and made pursuant to section 53 of the Employment Protection (Consolidation) Act 1978 we give you notice that the reason for your dismissal was:

After oral and three written notices you were persistently in breach of your contract of employment by ignoring the hours of work specified in your contract of employment.

dated 25 January 1991

Company Secretary

6.5 Summary dismissal

The most difficult dismissal to defend at an industrial tribunal is one for gross misconduct where the employee has been summarily dismissed. The employer must show that he or she has reasonable grounds to believe that the employee has done the action that gives rise to the dismissal. The employee should be given an opportunity to explain his or her conduct, and the employer must show that the continued employment is not in the best interests of the business (*James* v. *Waltham Holy Cross UDC*, 1973 ICR 398). As an example, the employee might appear to be drunk. Whether he or she was drunk or ill the employer cannot know from first impression. If the employer dismissed the employee without further enquiry the employer runs the risk of losing a defence to a claim for unfair dismissal. If the employer had followed the basic procedure and sent the employee home on a twenty-four hour suspension, invited him or her back next day to explain his/her condition and, if the explanation was unsatisfactory, then taken the decision to dismiss, the result would be different. Where, following a breach that justifies instant dismissal, it is decided to dismiss, Letter 62 would be appropriate. It is as well in these cases to spell out clearly why the conduct complained of is considered to be so grave as to justify instant dismissal. Letter 31 makes clear that the dismissal was because of the flagrant disregard of safety conditions that imperilled the safety of all in the building. Letter 62 makes it clear that what has been done was, firstly, a potentially criminal offence and, secondly, an action that rendered the employee incapable of performing his/her duties.

Letter 62

Letter giving summary dismissal

Dear James Brown

Yesterday you were found in the Managing Director's car quite incapable of speech and when asked to get out, you were unable to stand up. You were unable to speak properly and your breath smelled strongly of drink. You were sent home and this morning when asked for an explanation you said that at lunch you had been with others celebrating the birthday of Thomas Smith. In short, you were drunk.

You are employed as chauffeur for the Managing Director and the seriousness of your conduct cannot be overemphasised. Firstly, you were drunk in charge of the Managing Director's car. That is a criminal offence for which, had the police been involved, you would in all probability have been charged. Secondly, because of your condition you could not possibly have fulfilled your duties.

In the circumstances we feel that we have no alternative but to discharge you forthwith.

Yours sincerely

Personnel Manager

6.6 Effect of termination on an employee's DSS benefits

If an employee is dismissed for misconduct, his or her rights to benefit under the social security legislation can be called into question. Under the social security rules, benefit is not payable for an avoidable loss of employment. Cases where the employee is dismissed for sickness or for inability to perform the duties of the employment are not regarded as 'avoidable' and, accordingly, where an employee is dismissed for either of those two reasons, the correspondence should make it clear and so protect the position for the employee.

Letters 13, 14 and 15 indicate the path that must be followed in the case of sickness. From a moral point of view, this is possibly the most difficult of situations for an employer to face. If an employee has a health problem and is subject to an unreasonable amount of time off or an extended period of sickness-related absence, the employer should be extremely slow to dismiss and the procedure outlined in Section 3.2 should be followed. If, following the further medical examination that Letter 15 envisages action to terminate the employment has to be considered, before making a dismissal the employee must be consulted, otherwise the dismissal is unfair. First write Letter 63.

Letter 63

Letter to sick employee

Dear

We have now received a report from our doctor following his examination of you. His views support entirely those of your own doctor.

We are extremely concerned as to your continued absence through ill health. You are out of time so far as the employer's statutory sick pay scheme is concerned and you must now rely upon the DSS.

You will realise that the Company has to keep the situation under constant review. We are most reluctant to consider terminating your employment but have to have regard to the fact that your work has to be done and that your absence is placing an unfair workload on your colleagues. I very much fear that your illness is going to mean that your absence will be prolonged and that you will not be able to return soon. We will have to consider replacing you which means that we shall have to terminate your employment. Before we take this step, we would like to see you and discuss it with you. If you are not well enough to come to the office here, ask someone to telephone for you and I will come and see you.

Yours sincerely

When it becomes apparent to the employer that the absence can no longer be accepted, a termination of the contract of employment can be made by Letter 64.

Letter 64

Termination of employment for long-term sickness

Dear

It is with real regret that the Company has now taken the decision to terminate your employment. This letter is to notify you that your employment will end in   weeks' time. [The appropriate period of notice – see Section 6.3 – must be given.] The only reason for our terminating your contract is your health.

But for the fact that your incapacity has proved such a difficulty for you and for the Company, we would be delighted to retain you as a valued and loyal employee. When your health recovers to allow you to resume work, we would be very pleased to re-engage you. You may, of course, give our name as a reference to any other employer, being confident that we would speak highly of your loyalty and, in good health, ability.

Yours sincerely

In the case of an employee who is found to be quite incapable of performing the duties for which he or she is engaged, the employer could offer other employment. That, though, could itself amount to a dismissal. All opportunities must be explored. The employer must be certain that the employee has been given all opportunity to make him- /herself fit to perform the required duties. The possibility of the employee taking other duties should be explored. Those other duties must be suitable alternative employment. You could not, to take an extreme example, offer a person who was engaged as a computer programmer the job of invoice clerk. In the case which is noted on p. 104, Sir John Donaldson (the presiding judge) said:

> If an employee is not measuring up to the job, it may be because he is not exercising himself sufficiently or it may be because he really lacks the capacity to do so. An employer should be very slow to dismiss upon the grounds that the employee is incapable of performing the work which he is employed to do, without first telling the employee of the respects in which he is failing to do his job adequately, warning him of the possibility or likelihood of dismissal on this ground, and giving him the opportunity of improving his performance.

Before taking action to dismiss for incompetence Letter 65 should be written.

Letter 65

First warning letter – incompetence

Dear

You have been employed as a   . On previous occasions your supervisor has warned you that you are not doing the work correctly and has tried to help you by showing you the way it should be done. It is apparent that you are not carrying out your work with the degree of competence that should be expected from someone who claims to have the experience that you claim to have.

We are willing to help you and if you want to have a period of instruction or guidance to enable you to increase your performance, please let me know. If we can, we will assist you.

You must take this letter as a warning that we are not satisfied with your level of competence and you must make every effort to improve.

Yours sincerely

If there is no satisfactory improvement following that letter, write Letter 66.

Letter 66

Second warning – incompetence

Dear

I wrote to you earlier telling you that we were not satisfied that you were performing your work with the degree of competence that was expected. You have not improved.

I must warn you that unless you improve, you are likely to be dismissed. I want you to have every opportunity and again offer to you the opportunity for further training and help. You must remember that others might be affected by your poor work, quite apart from its effect on the reputation of the company.

Yours sincerely

If there is no improvement, a last warning should be given.

Letter 67

Final warning – incompetence

Dear

In view of the fact that you have failed to improve your standards of work, and of the fact that I have given you two previous written warnings and offered to help you with training and help, I fear that there is no alternative for me but to give you this final warning. Unless your standards improve, you will be dismissed.

You have a right of appeal under your contract of employment and you can exercise that right at any time. If you feel that it would help you, I could arrange for you to be transferred to other work which might be more suited to your ability, and invite you to come and see me to discuss this possibility.

Yours sincerely

When all else has failed, then dismissal is inevitable – Letter 68.

Letter 68

Dismissal for incompetence

Dear

Since you have not been able, despite the offers of help, to raise your level of competence to an acceptable standard, and since there is no other employment with us that you could undertake, we have regretfully decided that your employment with us must be terminated. You must take this letter as   weeks' notice to this effect.

The reason for the dismissal is simply because you were quite obviously unable to perform the duties for which you were engaged. I am sure that you tried hard to make yourself competent, but the unhappy fact was that the work was quite beyond your capability.

If you wish to leave our employ before the expiry of the notice, I am sure that this could be arranged. If you wish to make any appeal against this decision under our disputes procedure, then you are, of course, free to do so.

Yours sincerely

It may be that instead of giving notice the employer would prefer to pay wages in lieu of notice. This topic is dealt with in Section 6.9 below.

6.7 Suspension

There is no right in common law for an employer to suspend an employee without pay. Only if the contract of employment expressly provides for suspension without pay can an employer lay off the workforce without paying them. The position was explained in Section 3.1 that the law now gives employees the statutory right to guaranteed basic payment and only if an employee refuses to undertake reasonable alternative work could that employee be laid off without pay. If the employer has no work of any kind to offer the employees or if, for example, the employer's lease came to an end and the works had to be vacated before new premises were ready for occupation, the employer could only lay off the workforce on full basic pay and that might be prohibitively expensive. The employer could make the workforce redundant but he or she might not want to do that. The closedown might be for a short period. Any suspension without pay would be a dismissal and could give rise to claims. It is an obvious case for negotiation with the workforce or the union (if any) representing them. There are special exceptions created by statute to the common law rule, where on health grounds the employer has to close the works or where in accordance with health and safety reasons the employer suspends the employee on medical grounds. In those cases the employee may be suspended (laid-off in lay terms) and an employee who has been in employment for at least one month then becomes entitled to pay for a maximum of twenty-six weeks. Letter 69 is the appropriate letter to write in those circumstances.

Letter 69

Lay-off for health reasons

To all employees

Following the explosion in the spirit shed we are advised that there is serious risk to health from the fumes that are still being emitted from the tanks. Work is proceeding as rapidly as possible to repair the damage and make the premises safe. [The important part of this paragraph is to make clear that the reason for the lay-off is a health and safety matter.]

Meanwhile, all employees are notified that they should not attend for work until further notice. All employees who have been employed by the Company for more than one month will receive full wages. Whilst we fully expect to complete the works of repair within the next two months, it is right that all should know that the entitlement to wages during this lay-off will end after twenty-six weeks.

6.8 Criminal activity

Where an employee is under investigation by the police for a possible criminal offence, either within or outside of the employment, then the employer must consider the implications for the company. If it is an in-house matter, then the employee will be dealt with through the measures expressed in the company's disciplinary procedures, possibly requiring a period of suspension pending the result of inquiries. Any suspension must be on full pay. Letter 70 should be written. Before the matter has reached the stage where this letter has to be written, the employee should have been interviewed, told of the suspicions and given an opportunity to explain. Only when the explanation is not accepted should the employer take the next step, which is to suspend the employee and report the matter to the police for investigation.

Letter 70

Letter of suspension for suspected criminal offence

Dear

We are not satisfied with the explanation that you gave this morning when we told you of our suspicions concerning   [set out the problem, e.g. 'the shortage in your cash book']. We propose to call in the police to investigate.

Pending the outcome of those investigations you are suspended from your duties and should not attend at these premises unless requested. You should not remove anything from your desk, not even your personal property. We expect you to co-operate fully with the police in their inquiries. For your sake, we hope that the inquiries will exonerate you from any suspicion.

Yours sincerely

If, however, the employee is under investigation by the police for some external matter that may not be directly related to the employment, the employer must take care in anything that is said or done. To say or imply that someone is guilty of a criminal offence can be defamatory and give rise to a civil claim. Even the fact that the employee is subsequently convicted is not an answer to a claim in libel or slander if the person defamed can show in the civil proceedings that the conviction was unsafe. Where the accusations made against the employee might have an effect upon the company (for example, allegations of improper sexual conduct made against a schoolmaster may well have a serious effect upon the reputation of the school), then the employer will want to suspend the employee until the matter has been resolved one way or another. Remember that everyone is presumed innocent until proved guilty, so proceed on the basis that the employee is innocent. Letter 71 could be written.

Letter 71

Letter suspending for suspected criminal offence not connected with the employment

Dear

I am very sorry to hear of the police inquiries that are being made into your affairs.

Whilst I am sure that they will eventually exonerate you from all blame, I am sure that you will realise the embarrassment that it is causing for the company.

In the circumstances, I think that it is better that you do not attend for work until the inquiries are complete and we know whether or not any charges will be brought against you.

You will, of course, be paid during this period of suspension.

Yours sincerely

Should the employee be committed to prison, then the employer should treat this as a breach of contract, not as a frustration of the contract. The view that has been taken by tribunals is that the employee must have brought the situation upon him- or herself. Frustrating matters are usually restricted to things like an opera singer losing his or her voice and being unable to fulfil an engagement. The employment is not automatically terminated. This is a case where instant dismissal would be justified. Letter 72 should be written.

Letter 72

Instant dismissal for criminal conviction

Dear

Following your conviction today and the sentence of imprisonment imposed on you by the Court, we can no longer continue your employment.

We consider that a conviction and sentence of this nature is a fundamental breach of your contract of employment and you are now dismissed from our employment.

Yours sincerely

6.9 Payment in lieu of notice

Apart from those cases where instant dismissal is appropriate, the dismissal always involves the giving of notice to determine the contract. An employer may well take the view that if the employee has to be asked to leave it would be better that he or she went at once and not wait for a period of notice to expire. Technically, if the employee is told to leave at once that would be a breach of contract by the employer and the damages that would result is the wages that would otherwise be earned by the employee during the notice period. It is for this reason that the employer would more often than not give wages in lieu of notice. Remember that it is not just the weekly wage that is due; there are other payments such as accrued holiday pay to consider. Of course, the warning procedure explained in Section 6.3 above must be followed before any dismissal. Letter 70 is an alternative form which could be used to replace the first paragraphs of Letters 61, 64 and 68. In each case the sentence in those letters referring to the giving of notice is deleted and the following paragraph written:

Letter 73

Making payment in lieu of notice

Dear

You are entitled to   weeks' notice but I feel that it is better that you leave at once. In the circumstances, your employment is terminated as from today. You will be paid your accrued pay to date, your accrued holiday pay to date and   weeks' wages in lieu of notice. A cheque for the amount due, together with a statement showing how it is made up, is enclosed.

Yours sincerely

6.10 Fixed term contracts

Fixed term contracts, that is to say contracts that expire on a defined date and not on the happening of a particular event (the giving of so many days', weeks' or months', notice for example) or the completion of a particular task, have certain statutory rights attached to them. The first is that an employee under a contract for a period of two years or more may agree in writing to renounce his or her rights to claim a redundancy payment or for unfair dismissal. The second is that, unless there has been an agreement of this nature, if the employee is not retained at the end of the term, he or she is deemed to have been dismissed and has either a redundancy claim or a claim for unfair dismissal, whichever is appropriate in the circumstances. Of course, the employee cannot be dismissed before the end of the term – that would be a straightforward breach of contract by the employer and would expose the employer to a claim for substantial damages. If the employer does not renew the contract his or her reasons will have to be justified. In any contract which is for a fixed term of two years or more (and such a contract should definitely be in writing, preferably a formal contract as in Document 2) there should be a clause on the lines of Document 8.

Document 8

Clause for a fixed term contract excluding rights to redundancy or unfair dismissal

The employee agrees for the purposes of section 142 of the Employment Protection (Consolidation) Act 1978 that the non-renewal of this agreement at the end of its term shall not be deemed to be a dismissal for the purposes of the employment legislation and that accordingly his rights to compensation for unfair dismissal and his rights to claim for redundancy are hereby excluded.

6.11 Redundancy

Economic and trading downturn in Britain has led to redundancy. To alleviate the condition of employees who lose their employment through no fault of their own, the Redundancy Payments Act 1965 was passed. This Act gives workers the right to the payment of a tax-free sum to compensate for loss of employment through redundancy. The amount payable depends upon the age and length of service of the employee. An employee who is over the normal retiring age is not entitled to a redundancy payment. Originally, the employer was entitled to recover 50 per cent of any payment from the government. This percentage has been reduced over the years and the right to a repayment is extinguished by the Wages Act 1989. In deciding how long an employee has been in continuous employment with the employer, time spent in the employment of an associated employer is taken into account. This is why in Document 1 it was necessary to say whether there was any employment with a previous employer which would count as part of the continuous employment. An employer may try to disguise dismissal of an employee and declare the employee redundant. The redundancy law requires the employer to show that there is a genuine economic or trading reason for the dismissal. The employer who wishes to close down one part of the business or who has decided on a rationalisation of the business or who has introduced new techniques that make the work being done unnecessary can dismiss employees on redundancy grounds. The correct guideline is not why the requirement for employment has ceased but the fact that it has. In any dispute this is what the employer must show. Where possible, if work of a similar nature exists in another part of the employer's business, the offer of alternative employment must be considered. Where the alternative employment is in a different location, the employee's contract of employment must be considered. It is not a case of where the employee worked but where he or she could be required to work. If the contract entitled the employer to move the employee from one site to another, then an offer of employment at the alternative site would exclude the redundancy. Letter 29 was suggested where an employee agreed to this, although the contract of employment did not compel him/her to do so, and was moved from one site to another. Letter 74 is a letter where an employee can be called upon to work at any of the employer's business premises.

Letter 74

Letter requiring a worker to move to a new workplace to avoid redundancy

Dear

As you have been informed, we have decided that because of adverse trading conditions it has become necessary for us to close down the filling station at Main Road, Newtown.

You will in future be transferred to the filling station at Planter Road where your duties, wages and conditions of employment will be exactly the same.

Yours sincerely

Assuming that the contract of employment requires the employee to work at any of the company's premises, a refusal to obey this instruction would not incur dismissal and if the employee left, he or she would not be entitled to redundancy.

Where it has become necessary to make employees redundant and no other employment can be offered, there should be discussion before taking action. If there is an agreement with the trade union establishing an agreed procedure on redundancy, this procedure must obviously be followed. Otherwise, selection of an employee for redundancy must be made on reasonable grounds. The employer does not have to justify his or her reasons for making employees redundant but does have to justify selection of any particular individual. 'Last in, first out' is the most usual basis for selection, but operating this system can mean that the employer is left with a workforce consisting mostly of elderly people. It was stated in the House of Lords decision noted above (Section 6.3):

> the employer will normally not act reasonably unless he warns and consults any employees affected or their representatives, adopts a fair basis upon which to select for redundancy and takes such steps as may be reasonable to avoid or minimise redundancy by redeployment within his own organisation.

'Last in, first out' has been recognised as a fair basis in many cases. If that is the basis of selection, then Letter 73 could be written to the selected employees.

Letter 75

Letter notifying redundancy

Dear

Following the discussions that we have had with all the workforce, as I told you this morning, it is with real regret that I have to tell you that because of the serious downturn in business there is no longer any work for you to do. For this reason, and only for this reason, I have to end your employment with us. You have been a good and loyal employee and I can only hope that the enclosed cheque, which represents your final pay, accrued holiday pay, four weeks' wages in lieu of notice and a redundancy payment, will help to tide you over until you find other work.

As you will have noticed for yourself, there has been a steady decline in orders and we have reached the point where we have no choice but to make some employees redundant. The principle that we have adopted following discussions with you all has been 'last in, first out'. I am sorry that others have been with us for a longer period and I have therefore had to include you amongst those made redundant.

You may rest assured that if at any time you need a reference you can always refer to me confident that the reference will be a good one.

Yours sincerely

6.12 Transfer of the business

The Transfer of Undertakings (Protection of Employment) Regulations 1981 require that where a business is sold and the purchaser agrees to buy the business as a 'going concern', then any persons who are employed by the original owner are 'transferred' with the business to the new owner. When a business is sold, the sale can take one of two different forms. Where the business operates as a limited company, the purchaser can either buy the shares, in which case, so far as employees are concerned, there is no change in their contract, or the sale takes the form of a sale of the assets of the business. An assets sale means that the purchaser will form a new company and the new company will buy the premises, plant, stock in trade, goodwill and any other assets that there may be. So far as the employees are concerned, their contracts are with the old company. If they are to work for the new one, new contracts will be required. The regulations provide that in those circumstances, even though there are on the face of it two different employers, the original contract is treated as having gone on without a break. In other words, there is continuous employment. A new statement of terms of employment, as in Document 1, should be issued but paragraph 3 will state the 'period of employment with [name of the previous employer] counts as part of your continuous employment'. Continuous employment is important because it is the number of years of continuous employment that have to be calculated for redundancy and also for calculating the number of weeks' notice required to end the contract. If the new company wants to change the terms of employment, then the position described in Section 1.7 must be considered and possibly Letter 5 written. If there is to be no change in the terms, then Letter 76 should be placed in the pay envelope of all employees.

Letter 76

Notice of change of ownership

On Friday 18 January 1991 the business of John Smith Limited was acquired by International Conglomerates PLC. A new Company has been formed, John Smith (1991) Limited, to carry on the business and this Company will be a part of the International Conglomerates Group.

The contracts of all employees are being transferred to that Company. There will be no changes to any of the terms of your employment but all employees will now have the benefit of the social and sports facilities enjoyed by all employees in the group.

CHAPTER 7

Discrimination and harassment

7.1 Discrimination in the selection of employees

The Sex Discrimination Act 1975 and the Race Relations Act 1976 make it unlawful for anyone to discriminate against any person or persons on the grounds of colour, race, nationality or ethnic or national origins, or on the grounds of gender. The discrimination is forbidden both in the selection of applicants for employment and in the treatment of employees during employment. In any advertisement for employees, care must be taken not to indicate a prejudice. The regulations do not apply to any employment where being a member of a particular racial group, or being a member of a particular sex is a genuine occupational qualification for a job. For example, it is not discriminatory to advertise for a Chinese employee for a Chinese restaurant, nor for a woman as cloakroom attendant in a ladies' toilet. The qualification has to be a genuine reason for a real purpose. Where a genuine reason for requiring applicants to have the desired racial or sex qualification exists then the advertisement must be carefully worded to show why the requirement is being made and avoid any implications that the choice is being made for some improper discriminatory motive. Advertisements 7 and 8 are examples.

Advertisement 7

Advertisement for a genuine occupational qualification (Example 1)

Lady required as cook for girls' school

The St Margaret's School for Young Ladies is an all-girls boarding school for girls from the ages of 11 to 18. A residential cook is required due to the retirement of Mrs Beaton who has served the school well over the past 45 years. The applicant, who because this is an all-female school should be female, will be accommodated at the school and must be experienced in the preparation of traditional English meals and in the supervision of a kitchen serving 200 meals at a sitting. A pension scheme, generous leave entitlement, own apartment and an attractive salary will be offered. Apply to The Bursar, St Margaret's School for Young Ladies, Tonbridge Wells, Kent.

Advertisement 8

Advertisement for a genuine occupational qualification (Example 2)

Manager required for Indian restaurant

A manager is required for the Shere Khan Restaurant, Lewisham. The restaurant specialises in traditional Bengali cooking and is fully licensed for all alcoholic drinks. All employees at the present are native born Bengalis and the applicant should ideally also be a native born Bengali. Any applicant of an Indian ethnic origin will be considered for the position. Preference will be given to an applicant who has had experience in restaurant management in a high class restaurant with fifty tables.

Where the employment offered is capable of being performed by persons of either sex or of any racial origin, care must be taken to avoid any suggestion of discrimination. Advertisement 9 is an example of an alternative post being offered equivalent to that described in Advertisement 7 but without the need for a sex qualification.

Advertisement 9

Advertisement without sexual discrimination

Cook required for co-educational school

The St Margaret's School is a co-educational day school for pupils from the age of 11 to 18. A cook is required due to the retirement of Mrs Beaton who has served the school well over the past 45 years. The applicant (male or female) must be experienced in the preparation of traditional English meals and in the supervision of a kitchen serving 200 meals at a sitting. A pension scheme, generous leave entitlement, and an attractive salary will be offered. Apply to The Bursar, St Margaret's School, Tonbridge Wells, Kent.

Where the position offered involves work overseas, the restriction would not apply. An employment agency advertising for an employee to work in the Middle East, for example, might take account of the views of the community there and restrict the offer of employment to males. Women are not allowed to drive motor cars in Saudi Arabia. Advertisement 10 would be permissible. If the post offered was for employment solely in the United Kingdom, it would be discriminatory.

Advertisement 10

Advertisement for an overseas employee

Chauffeur wanted

Man required as chauffeur for Saudi Arabian Company. Must be Rolls Royce trained. The position will be for an initial term of two years and will be based in Riyadh. The selected applicant will be a teetotal non-smoker. Salary will be paid tax free. Six months' leave with return air fare will be given at the expiry of the contract. Generous salary, luxury accommodation and substantial bonus paid at the conclusion of the term. Apply Josiah Brown, The Middle East Recruitment Agency Ltd, St Thomas' Street, Parktown.

When applicants are being interviewed for employment, care must be taken not to give any indication of discrimination. Questions asked must be the same for all applicants. Particular care must be taken with questions related to religion. The Race Relations Act refers to discrimination on the grounds of race, not religion, but in the case of both Jews and Sikhs, their religion has also been considered by the Courts to establish an ethnic characteristic. Language alone does not characterise an ethnic group. So it was not considered to be discriminatory to advertise for 'A Welsh-speaking applicant' (*Gwynedd C. C.* v. *Jones* 1986 ICR 833). It would have been discriminatory to ask for 'a Welsh applicant' since that was directly referring to nationality. Document 9 is a check list for interviews.

Document 9

Check list for interviews

Name
Address

Education
Educational/professional/technical qualifications
Languages spoken
Previous employment since leaving school
Last employment
Reasons for leaving
Marital status
Dependants
Health
Number of days sick or off work in last twelve months
Reasons
Smoker or non-smoker
Hobbies and outside interests
Reasons for applying for the position offered
Trade union membership
Questions where race or sex is a problem:
   any strong feelings on religion or race
   any objection to working in a mixed workforce
   any previous experience of discrimination or harrassment

When the selection for employment has been made, an offer of employment will be sent to the successful applicant, Letters 1 and 2 being examples. The unsuccessful applicants should also be written to and told why they have been unsuccessful. In this letter the opportunity should be taken to dispel any suspicion that either sex or race played any part in the selection. Letter 77 is an example of the sort of letter that could be written.

Letter 77

Letter to an unsuccessful applicant

Dear

Thank you for applying for the post of manager and for sparing the time to come for interview.

   I am very sorry to have to disappoint you by telling you that we have decided to appoint another applicant. The choice was a difficult one to make because of the high standard of all applicants. The person chosen had the advantage of many more years' experience in this type of work and could, in addition, offer other skills.

Had it not been for this, it is probable that we would have offered the position to you.

Again my thanks for your application; should a further position of this nature occur, I will communicate with you to see whether you are interested.

Yours sincerely

7.2 Discrimination in the course of employment

The difficulties of an employer do not end with the avoidance of any discriminatory attitudes or actions in the hiring of the employee; in the workplace there will be problems to be countered. People cannot be forced to like each other. The matter of indirect discrimination has to be considered and countered by the employer wherever possible. Indirect discrimination can take many forms, one of which will be to create difficulties for persons of different race and ethnic origin who are seeking promotion. There are many cases of industrial tribunal applications that have originated through an employer's tacit and unexplained refusal to promote an otherwise suitable applicant to a higher position with the only reason, so far as the applicant has suspected, for the refusal being based upon race or sex. The employer, faced with an application to a tribunal, must show why the applicant was not chosen for promotion or a particular course of training. The employer will have to be sure that the company policy with regard to the equality of all employees within the workplace is strictly enforced, recognised and well-known to all. Promotion within the organisation must be on merit and ability with no question of race or sex having any bearing. The employer's motives or less favourable treatment, be they good, bad or indifferent, are irrelevant. If the action does discriminate, it is unlawful. Men were considered to have been subjected to unlawful discrimination when only men were chosen to work in very dirty conditions, the employer excluding women because he thought it could affect their hair. A woman was discriminated against when an employer refused to employ her because he genuinely believed that, from his previous experience, it was unwise for her to be the only woman in the group. If a choice has to be made between applicants for advancement or for some special treatment such as a training or instructional course, and the question of race or sex could arise, then the reasons for the choice should be made clear. It would be usual for the manager responsible for making the choice to see the candidates and explain to them about the decision taken. If a course of instruction were offered, or if volunteers were being invited to apply for some privileged working conditions, then Letter 75 would be the sort of notice to give to all employees. The point being made is that the basic qualifications for consideration must be made known so that when a decision has to be made a clear division can be achieved between those who are qualified and those who are not.

Letter 78

Notice inviting employees to apply for a course

The Company will be offering to send certain employees on a week's course at the Cranfield College of Management. The course is designed to increase skills in marketing and selling and will run from 11 February to 17 February.

There will be ten places offered. Those chosen must have been with the Company for not less than three years and they will be senior sales employees who have demonstrated their success in selling by their sales figures over the past twelve months. If more than ten apply, those with the highest numbers of sales over the twelve months to 31 December last will be chosen.

Please make a written application giving your reasons why you think that you should be chosen rather than any other applicant. In the event that there will be two or more applicants with the same sales results for last year, the persuasiveness of the reasons given will be used to judge between them.

Sales Director

7.3 Sex discrimination and sexual harassment

The Sex Discrimination Act 1975 seeks to prevent discrimination against either sex, although the emphasis is usually on the female. The Act deals with all aspects in life, not just employment. Discrimination may be direct, as where an employee is refused employment or advancement because of his or her sex; indirect, as where conditions are imposed which are such that a considerably smaller proportion of people of one sex can comply with it; or sexual harrassment. Direct discrimination is easily perceived. Indirect discrimination is more difficult to detect. As an example, the Civil Service Commission imposed a condition that applicants for executive officer should be between the ages of seventeen-and-a-half and twenty-eight years. A female applicant aged thirty-six successfully challenged this condition on the basis that between these ages many women would be unable to take up employment because that was the time when they would be bearing children or having young children to mind. After an appeal, the Commission conceded that because of this fact the number of women who would be able to satisfy the condition was fewer than men. The condition was an indirect discrimination. When imposing conditions of employment, the danger must be kept in mind. The reasons for the Civil Service condition was that they wished to create a proper career structure. It would have been unexceptional if they had prescribed a minimum age (say seventeen years) and not a maximum. When drafting conditions for employment, a distinction is drawn between those conditions which are a 'must' and those characteristics which will be taken into account as favourable and unfavourable. Once employed, the Act makes unlawful any action taken by an employer that is detrimental to the employee if the action is taken on the grounds of sex. So, refusal of promotion, imposition of working rules, or the refusal of privileges granted to other employees can cause an offence under the Act.

When advertising or making an offer of employment, selecting for redundancy, or granting or refusing privileges for employees, the check list in Document 10 lists some of the conditions or considerations that have been held to be discriminatory.

Document 10

Check list of discriminatory conditions

- Single person only (or no married person) – discriminates against married people.
- No persons with young children – will affect more married persons than unmarried and more women.
- Must work full time – will affect more women than men.
- Pension provisions for women at sixty years and men at sixty-five years. Must retire on becoming entitled to State retirement pension – women get the pension at sixty years and men at sixty-five years.

Harassment has been recognised as a form of sexual discrimination. It must be understood that, although much more usually associated with male harrassment of the female, the male can also be subjected to this treatment. The young lad employed in a shop of woman operatives can experience just as much sexual innuendo and 'teasing' as the female typist, the 'traditional' target. An employer is liable for acts of sexual harrassment which are committed by one of his/her employees if the harassment was done 'in the course of ... employment'. In other words, if the Sales Director makes improper approaches to his secretary whilst they are at work, the employer can be responsible. The Act says that anything done by a person in the course of his/her employment shall be treated for the purposes of the Act as done by the employer as well as by the employee, whether or not it was done with the employer's knowledge and approval. To protect themselves employers must prove that such steps as were reasonably practicable were taken to prevent an employee from behaving in the manner about which the complaint has been made. Where an employer has reason to believe that some form of harassment has taken place, action should be taken at once. Since evidence is going to be needed to prove that action was taken, it is best that there is a written record. Letter 79 is the form in which such evidence could be provided.

Letter 79

Letter warning about harassment conduct

Dear

This letter is a formal record of the warning and reprimand that was given to you this morning. It was reported to me by Miss Robinson that you touched her in a familiar manner, attempted to kiss her and made improper suggestions that she could advance her career prospects by giving you sexual favours.

When you were told of these suggestions you attempted to excuse your conduct by saying that she encouraged you. Whether or not this was so, your conduct is inexcusable. Having seen and interrogated you both, I am satisfied that Miss Robinson did nothing to encourage you.

You must take this letter as a formal warning that no form of sexual or other harassment will be tolerated. Any repetition may result in dismissal.

Yours sincerely

On the other footing, where harassment is of a male by females, complaints are less likely to occur. The isolated male can find himself in a difficult position in a workplace that is dominated by females who can, in some cases, sexually harass that male. The typical masculine reaction to such harassment – 'he should be so lucky' – is no proper response. The male is entitled to the same protective legislation as the female. Even at the risk of adding to the embarrassment of the male concerned, action should be taken. Make the action with some discretion. A notice in the wage packet might be appropriate.

Letter 80

Notice of sexual harassment of a male employee

It has come to our notice that innuendos and suggestions concerning John's masculinity are being regularly made. Teasing of a sexual nature cannot be tolerated. John has made no complaint and has taken the teasing in good part. Just as none of our female employees are expected to tolerate sexual harassment, so we expect to protect employees who are placed in John's position from this unpleasant conduct. The teasing and sexual approaches to John must cease. Anyone who is heard or found to be indulging in this sort of behaviour must anticipate disciplinary action being taken against them.

CHAPTER 8

Employee benefits

8.1 Motor vehicles

There are many fringe benefits offered to employees, of which probably the most usual is the company car. Here, an employee is taxed according to a scale which depends on the age and engine size of the car. The taxation, compared with the cost of buying and running a car, gives a considerable advantage to an employee such that the provision of a car has become almost a standard part of every employment package. The contract of employment should always have a clause related to the provision of a car and the rules as to its use (see clause 6 of Document 2 and particularly clause 6(c)). A specimen of the regulations which could be envisaged is in Document 11.

Document 11

Regulations controlling car usage

1. The car will at all times be available for inspection by a duly authorised representative of the Company. The car will be returned to the Company on request being made by the Company or on the termination of the employee's contract of employment.
2. When not in use, the car will be secured with all windows closed and all doors locked. Whilst left at the employee's residence, the car will be kept in a locked garage.
3. The car will be regularly serviced in accordance with the manufacturer's recommendations by a reputable garage to be

approved by the Company. The cost of servicing will be at the Company's/employee's expense.

4. Any defects or breakdown of the car will immediately be reported to the Company and a full note made of the defect or breakdown to enable the Company to make claim under the warranty given to the Company on its purchase of the car.

5. Any damage suffered by the car or any incident that may give rise to a claim being made against the Company or the employee will be immediately reported to the Company and a written report made on the incident. The employee will co-operate with the Company and its insurers in any claim that may arise.

6. The car will not be driven at any time that the employee is unfit, whether through drink, ill-health or any other reason.

7. The employee will not use the car in any way that could or might invalidate the insurance policy effected by the Company.

8. The car will not, without the prior written consent of the Company, be taken out of the United Kingdom.

9. No person other than the employee shall be allowed to drive the car except in cases of emergency. The employee will not use the car in any way at any time when he or she is disqualified from driving or does not have in force a valid licence to drive the car.

10. The employee will be personally liable for all fines for any violation of any traffic laws, any fines or charges made for unlawful parking or breach of parking bye-laws.

The provision of a company car for an employee is a useful way to give an employee a tax advantaged benefit. The provision of the car does involve tax for the employee, tax that is based upon the value, age and size of car. The taxable value of the car is not increased if the employer pays all the charges involved: repairs, insurance, road tax and all other expenses of keeping the car on the road. Even if fuel is paid for by the employer (that is subject to tax, although again based upon a scale depending upon car value and size), the value to the employee is probably greatly in excess of the taxable value. As a result an employer might reasonably reward an employee by giving the privilege of a car as part of an increased salary package. Where an employee's contract of employment has no provision for a company car and the employee is subsequently given that extra privilege, his or her contract of employment has to be considered. A new clause relating to the car is added. If the vehicle is to be kept at the employee's home and is intended to be used only for business purposes, Letter 81 is appropriate. If the employee is intended to have full, unrestricted use, then Letter 82 applies.

Letter 81

Clause relating to a company car

The employee will be provided with a company car which is intended to be used only for the purpose of enabling the employee to travel to and from the Company's premises and otherwise on the business of the Company. The employee will:

1. At all times conform with all regulations which may from time to time be imposed by the Company in regard to motor cars provided by the Company for its employees.
2. Not without the previous consent of the Company use the vehicle otherwise than for the business of the Company and for the purpose of travelling to and from the Company's premises.
3. Provide the Company with vouchers and receipts for all fuel, repairs and other expenses incurred by him or her in respect of the vehicle.

The Company will

1. Keep the vehicle taxed and insured under an insurance which will permit the employee to use the car on the road.
2. Pay all costs and expenses incurred in respect of repairs, insurance, road tax, and all other expenses of keeping the car on the road and will reimburse the employee against the production of receipts and vouchers for any expenses incurred in connection with those expenses, or of fuel purchased for the proper use of the car.

Any misuse of the vehicle or breach of these conditions shall be a breach of the of the employee's contract of employment and be dealt with under the rules and disciplinary procedures of the Company.

Letter 82

Clause permitting unlimited use of company car

The employee will be provided with a company car for his or her use whilst on the Company's business or for personal pleasure.

The employee will:

1. At all times conform with all regulations which may from time to time be imposed by the Company in regard to motor cars provided by the Company for its employees.
2. Provide the Company with vouchers and receipts for all fuel, repairs and other expenses incurred by him/her in respect of the vehicle.

The Company will:

1. Keep the vehicle taxed and insured under an insurance which will permit the employee to use the car on the road.
2. Pay all costs and expenses incurred in respect of repairs, insurance, road tax and all other expenses of keeping the car on the road and will reimburse the employee against the production of receipts and vouchers for any expenses he or she has incurred in connection with those expenses or of fuel purchased for the proper use of the car.

Any misuse of the vehicle or breach of these conditions shall be a breach of the employee's contract of employment and be dealt with under the rules and disciplinary procedures of the Company.

8.2 Private health insurance

There is a benefit to the employer in ensuring that employees are able to receive medical treatment at times that are convenient to them and the business and that an employee can obtain treatment speedily and without waiting for treatment to become available under the National Health. An employee crippled by arthritis will underperform whilst he or she waits for a hip operation. For this reason many employers are now offering employees the benefit of private medical insurance. When this benefit is introduced those employees who are offered the privilege must have special provisions offered to them. The problem for the employer is to cover the position where, for one reason or another, the benefit is withdrawn. The benefit has to be offered in such a way that it does not become a part of the contract of employment. That way, when it is withdrawn it does not raise the question of a dismissal. Letter 83 would be appropriate.

Letter 83

Notice that a BUPA scheme is available

The Company has negotiated with BUPA a group insurance for the benefit of nominated employees and their dependants. I am pleased to tell you that we are willing to nominate you as one of the employees to have the advantage of the scheme. The Company will pay all the premiums for the benefit and will not ask for any contribution from you. [If the employee is being asked to contribute, then say 'You will be asked to contribute £   per month towards this expense.]

I enclose a copy of the leaflet from BUPA describing the benefits offered and the procedure for claiming benefit. Please let me know whether you wish to be included in the scheme.

I must make it clear to you that this benefit is not intended to be a part of your contract of employment and that, whilst it is envisaged that this will be a permanent part of our general policy of good management relations with all our employees, we reserve the right to withdraw from the scheme at any time.

8.3 Share option schemes

It is becoming increasingly the case that companies offer their senior employees an option to purchase shares in the company.

This can be done quite informally, but in that case the employee can find a heavy tax burden. The alternative, of creating an approved scheme, will enable options to be granted to employees (although normally only offered to senior employees there is no reason why the option could not be offered to all) in a manner that avoids the tax disadvantages of an unapproved scheme. The topic is complicated and beyond the scope of this book. Once adopted, there are a number of letters and documents that will have to be written. The employer contemplating a scheme will have to take professional advice on its establishment and on obtaining Revenue approval. Once approved and ready to be implemented, the first task is to inform those who will be invited to participate. Letter 84 is appropriate.

Letter 84

Invitation to apply for a share option

10 January 1991

Dear

The Conglomerates Ltd executive share option scheme

1. The Board of Directors of the Company has decided to establish a scheme to enable selected executives to apply for an option to purchase shares in the Company. The Inland Revenue has given its approval to the scheme. I enclose a copy of the rules of the scheme which you should read carefully.

2. I am pleased to inform you that the Board have decided to invite you to apply for an option under the scheme in respect of 1,000 ordinary shares of £1 each (fully paid). I enclose a form which, if you wish to apply for an option under the scheme, you should complete and return to me as soon as possible. If I do not receive this form back within fourteen days of the date of this letter this invitation will be deemed to have been refused and the invitation will lapse. For technical legal reasons some consideration has to be given by you for the option, so when the

form is returned you must enclose a remittance of £1 with the application.

3. If you do apply, your application will be subject to acceptance by the Board. Any option granted will be subject to the terms and conditions of the scheme. The price payable per share under the option will be the market value of the Company's ordinary shares at the time of the grant. We have agreed with the share valuation division of the Inland Revenue that it will agree the value of the sum of £1.50 per share. If an option is granted to you, you will be given an option certificate confirming the date of the grant and stating the terms upon which it can be exercised and the price payable per share. When the option is exercised this certificate will have to be surrendered to the Company.

4. You must read the rules carefully. If there is anything that you do not understand, I will endeavour to explain it to you. You must particularly notice Rule 4. Except in the special circumstances noted in sub-paragraphs (ii) to (vii) inclusive of that rule, you will not be able to exercise the option until three years after it has been granted. You do not have to exercise the option in respect of all the shares offered and can, if you wish, take some in three years' time and more three years later. The whole option will lapse in respect of any shares not taken within ten years of the grant of the option.

5. The Board of Directors has confirmed to the Inland Revenue that in respect of any shares that are taken under the option they will not exercise their rights under the Articles of Association of the Company so as to discriminate against the transfer of any shares allotted under the scheme.

6. The Board of Directors is exercising the power given by Rule 2(c) to impose conditions on the exercise of the option. They will make a condition that the option will only be exercisable if the average profits earned by the company for the three financial years of the Company (the financial year of the Company ends on 31 December) 1990, 1991 and 1992 exceeds £500,000.

7. As mentioned above, the scheme has been approved by the Inland Revenue. As the law stands at the moment (tax law can, and frequently does, change every year) the tax treatment of options under approved schemes such as this is:
(a) No tax charge arises as a result of the grant of the option.

(b) If the option is exercised under the rules of the scheme, no income tax charge will arise provided at least three years have elapsed since the grant of the option or the exercise of the option granted by the scheme or any other approved scheme.

(c) The exercise by the personal representative of a deceased optionholder does not give rise to an income tax charge provided that the exercise is within ten years of the grant of the option.

(d) If the option is exercised in any other circumstances, an income tax charge will arise. So if the Directors were to give consent to the exercise of the option under paragraph 4 (vii), an income tax charge would arise. This charge is calculated on the difference between the market value of the shares at the date when the option is exercised and the price actually paid for them under the option.

(e) If the shares are disposed of after the option has been exercised, depending upon your financial circumstances, a charge to capital gains tax could arise.

Yours sincerely

Company Secretary

Application for an option
Pursuant to the invitation contained in your letter of 10 January 1991, I hereby apply for the grant to me of an option to acquire 1,000 ordinary shares of £1 each (fully paid) at the option price of £1.50 per share.

I have read and understood the rules of Conglomerate's executive share option scheme and I make this application subject to the terms of those rules and the condition referred to in paragraph 6 of the letter dated 10 January 1991.

I enclose my cheque for £1, the consideration payable for the grant of the option.

Dated this   January 1991

Following from the application, the Board will meet and resolve to grant options. Then a letter has to be written to the employee telling him or her that the application is successful and enclosing an option certificate, Letter 85.

Letter 85

Letter with option certificate

Dear

The Conglomerates Ltd executive share option scheme

I am pleased to tell you that the Board has considered your application to be granted an option to acquire shares under the share option scheme.

I enclose the certificate of the grant of the option. You should keep this and the rules of the scheme safely. If you exercise the option, you must produce this certificate. To help you, I enclose a form of letter exercising the option which you can use when the time comes. I remind you that the option cannot be exercised before 21 January 1994 (three years after the date of the option) except in the very special circumstances stated in Rule 4.

You should disclose this option in your next tax return.

Yours sincerely

Company Secretary

First enclosure:
The Conglomerates Ltd executive share option scheme

THIS IS TO CERTIFY

That pursuant to the provisions of the Conglomerates Ltd executive share option scheme and in consideration of the sum of £1

JOSHUA MARTIN FELLOWS

is hereby granted the option, subject to the provisions of the scheme and to the condition stated hereunder, to acquire 1,000

ordinary shares of £1 each (fully paid) in the capital of Conglomerates International Limited at the price of £1.50 per share.

This option is granted on the condition that

(a) It may not be exercised before 21 January 1994 and will lapse
    on 21 January 2001; and
(b) The option may only be exercised if the average profits earned
    by the Company for the three financial years of the Company
    (the financial year of the Company ends on the 31 December)
    1990, 1991 and 1992 exceeds £500,000.

Dated this   January 1991

Director

Second enclosure:
To the Directors
Conglomerates International Limited

Gentlemen

The Conglomerates Ltd executive share option scheme

Pursuant to Rule 5 of the above mentioned scheme, I hereby give
notice to exercise my option to acquire   ordinary shares of £1
each (fully paid) at the price of £1.50 per share.

I enclose my cheque for £   , the price payable, and the
option certificate.

Yours faithfully

When the time comes for the exercise of the option, the
employee will write the suggested form of letter and following
from that an allotment of shares will be made. If the option has
been exercised for only part of the shares, the certificate will be
endorsed 'option exercised in respect of shares on the day of
19   ', and returned together with the share certificate for
those shares taken (Letter 86).

Letter 86

Letter returning option certificate

Dear

I enclose the share certificate for the 500 shares allotted to you following the exercise of your option. You should keep this certificate in a safe place. If the shares are transferred you will have to hand over the certificate to the purchaser or, if only part of the shares are transferred, the certificate will have to be surrendered so that a new certificate can be issued for the balance of shares which you retain.

I also enclose the option certificate which has been endorsed. I remind you that you cannot exercise the option in respect of the remainder of the shares for another three years and unless you exercise it before 2001 (ten years after the option was originally granted) you will lose all rights.

Yours sincerely

8.4 Profit sharing schemes

Employers often want to give their employees an incentive by offering them some form of profit sharing arrangement and by making them feel part of the company in the same way as any shareholder is a part. If the scheme is some form of bonus arrangement under which the employee receives extra payment depending upon the profits earned by the business, the employee will have this payment treated, so far as tax is concerned, as if it were just part of his or her pay and will have no feeling that he/she has any say in the running of the company. It is possible for a profit sharing scheme to be adopted under the provisions of the Taxes Act under which the employee can have shares allocated to him or her without having any income tax to pay and become a full shareholder in the company. The scheme works like this:

A trust deed is executed and trustees are appointed. Either at the outset or when the company comes to consider declaring a dividend, the directors decide to allocate a proportion of profits earned to the trustees. The trustees use the moneys paid to them to purchase shares in the company which they hold in trust for the employees. Every employee has to be treated equally. They do not have to have the same number of shares – a differential can be made according to the salary status. Once the shares are allocated amongst the employees, if an employee does not sell the shares for five years, then there is no income tax payable. Effectively, the share of profit which has been used to buy the shares has been received by the employee free of tax. It is a complicated matter to describe. There are limits on the amount that can be allocated and the employee is not able to sell the shares for two years. If he or she sells at between two and five years, tax at a reducing scale could be payable. A company should take professional advice before adopting a scheme which must be approved by the Revenue to be effective. When a scheme is established, employees must be given the opportunity to say whether or not they wish to participate. Letter 87 is a letter to employees, explaining the scheme and inviting them to participate.

Letter 87

Letter inviting participation in profit sharing scheme

We have for some time been considering some way in which employees may share in the profit of the Company and become more involved as shareholders. We do not want to embark upon some arrangement which will cause more taxation problems. If a payment is made to employees it will, in the ordinary way, form part of their remuneration and be subject to tax at the highest rate of the individual employee. To enable employees to share in the profitability of the Company without incurring this tax burden, we have been advised to establish a Revenue approved scheme.

This is complicated to describe. What it amounts to is this. A trust has been established. From time to time, when the Board of Directors considers the dividend to be paid to the shareholders, they will allocate a proportion of the profits earned to the trustees. The trustees will use that money to buy shares in the Company. Those shares will be allocated to the employees. Although in this letter I am describing them as 'employee shares' they are in fact ordinary shares in the Company and will in all respects be the same as all other shares. They will give the right to vote and to share in profits.

All employees who have been with the Company for more than five years will be entitled to be part of the scheme. The trustees will allocate the shares to the employees individually. That means that each employee taking part in the scheme will be the same as any other shareholder. All of this can be done without any income tax being paid on the money that has been allocated PROVIDED THAT THE SHARES ARE NOT SOLD FOR TWO YEARS. After two years the shares can be sold, but then tax would be payable unless they are held for another three years, that is to say, five years in all. If they are not sold for five years, then no tax is payable. This will not be a 'one off' operation; every time that the Company's profits are considered, consideration will be given to making a payment to the trustees so that more and more shares can be purchased for the employees who are participating in the scheme.

The number of shares that each employee may be allocated on each occasion that the trustees have funds to invest is subject to a limit imposed by the Revenue. At present the limit is: if you are earning less than £20,000 per year, the limit is £2,000; if you are earning more than £20,000 per year the limit is 10 per cent of earnings up to a maximum of £6,000. Subject to the profits earned being sufficient, it is intended to allocate to each employee the maximum permitted.

As explained, for two years there can be no dealings with the shares – they must be left in the hands of the trustees. After two years, the employee can ask for the shares to be transferred to him or her. In that case, because there is a possibility that the shares could be sold with an income tax liability (remember the shares must be held for five years to escape income tax), the employee must pay the trustees a sum of money which represents this potential tax liability. This is because the trustees could become liable for the tax themselves and must be protected.

There is an exception to the rule that shares cannot be sold for five years. Any employee who dies whilst still employed, or any employee who retires whether because he or she has reached normal retirement age or has been forced to do so through sickness or disability, may ask for the shares to be sold and the proceeds paid over. There will be tax to pay, but only one half of the amount that would otherwise become due. If an employee leaves the Company before the two-year period has passed, the shares will continue to be held, but after two years the shares will be sold and, subject to tax being paid, the proceeds of the sale will be paid over.

So long as the shares are held, any dividends will be paid to the employee entitled. If the Company were to make a bonus issue of shares, the new shares would be added to the employee's shares. If there is any shareholders meeting, the trustees will ask the employee how he or she wants to vote on any question, and the trustees will vote accordingly. If nothing is said, then the trustee will not vote at all.

I enclose a copy of the trust document and of the rules. You are invited to say whether or not you would like to be part of the scheme. If you have any questions or doubts, let me know and I will try to help. It is a condition made by the Revenue that if you wish to join in the scheme you must sign and return to me the enclosed agreement.

One thing that I must make absolutely clear is that taking part in this scheme is quite separate from your contract of employment. You can join in or not absolutely as you wish. Whichever you do will in no way affect any rights or entitlements that you may have under your employment contract. If you leave the Company for any reason then the question of this scheme is irrelevant and will not be taken into consideration in calculating any claim that you may have. Equally so, the Company may, so long as it acts in accordance with the provisions of the scheme, alter, amend or wind up the scheme.

I await hearing from you.

Enclosure
Conglomerates Ltd profit sharing scheme

I apply to be allowed to participate in the approved profit sharing scheme. I confirm that I have read the rules of the scheme and I undertake with the Company and as a separate undertaking with the trustees of the scheme:

(a) that I will allow the shares to remain in the hands of the trustees during the period of detention named in the rules;

(b) that I will not assign, charge or otherwise dispose of my beneficial interest in the shares allocated to me during that period;

(c) that if at any time I direct the trustees to dispose of the shares before the release date defined in the rules, I will pay to the trustees before the transfer takes place a sum equal to income tax at the basic rate on the appropriate locked in value as defined in the rules of the shares at the time of the direction; and

(d) that I will not direct the trustees to dispose of the shares before the release date as defined in the rules in any other way except by sale for the best consideration in money that can reasonably be obtained at the time of sale.

Dated this   day of   19   .

Signed _____

When shares are allocated, the trustees must write to each participating employee telling him or her how many shares have been allocated and what is the amount of the holding to date. When shares are allocated at different dates, some will become free from selling restrictions whilst others cannot yet be sold. This must be made clear. A statement such as Letter 88 is appropriate.

Letter 88

Statement of allocated shares

A	B	C	D
No. of shares now allocated	No. of shares held for less than 2 years including column A	No. of shares held between 2 and 5 years	No. of shares held over 5 years
100	150	200	100

N.B.You are now free to deal with the shares in Column D, free from any restrictions under the scheme.

When there is a shareholders' meeting, the trustees will receive notice and must ask the employees how they want their votes to be cast (Letter 89).

Letter 89

Letter on shareholders' meeting

We have received notice of the annual general meeting of the Company to be held on 28 February. A copy of the agenda is enclosed. Will you please indicate on the enclosed form how you wish your vote to be cast on the various resolutions. You will notice Special Resolution 5 which relates to an increase in the Company's share capital. A copy of the notice that accompanied this agenda is enclosed so that you can see the reasons why the Board of Directors considers this necessary. In this Company, increase of capital requires a special resolution, which means that it must be passed by a 75 per cent majority. If we do not receive any indication at all from you, we will not vote on your behalf at the meeting.

Enclosure
Voting intention form

I wish my votes in respect of the resolutions to be proposed at the annual general meeting of the Company to be cast as follows:

Resolution 1.   To receive the report and accounts   Yes
   No

Resolution 2.   To declare a dividend   Yes
   No

Resolution 3.   To re-elect Mr Smith a Director   Yes
   No

Resolution 4.   To re-appoint auditors   Yes
                                                     No

Resolution 5.   To increase the share capital   Yes
                                                     No

Please tick 'Yes' or 'No' to indicate your wishes.

8.5 ESOP

For completeness, when considering the ways in which employees may be enabled to take an interest in their employer's
business, mention should be made of employee share ownership
plans (ESOPs for short). There is always a difficulty for anyone
who owns shares in a private company in selling the shares. It is
usual to find that the company's Articles of Association prevent
the free transfer of shares and often say that shares can only be
transferred to an existing shareholder. Moreover, a minority
shareholder has little or no say in the running of the business
and cannot compel the directors to let him or her have a seat on
the board. To give an employee shares in such a company is to
give very little. The employee cannot turn those shares into
money. In all possibility, the directors will see that the profits of
the company are used in such a way that little if any dividends
are paid to shareholders. How can this be overcome? The
company that wishes to benefit shareholders in such a way as to
avoid these disadvantages can consider an ESOP. What happens
is this. At the outset, a trust deed is established. The trustees,
either from funds given to them by the company or by an
arrangement with a bank (this is often a machinery used where
the company wishes to raise fresh capital), obtain the necessary
funds to subscribe for shares in the company. The trustees then
offer those shares for sale to employees. The trust deed sets out
the conditions as to the working of the trust. To be tax efficient
from the point of view of the company and the employees, the
scheme will have to satisfy the Revenue requirements. This
means that all employees will have to be enabled to take part,
the trustees must be at least three in number and one of them
must be a Trust Corporation, a solicitor or a member of some
other appropriate professional body. The majority of the trustees

must be employees (not directors) who have never held more than 5 per cent of the shares in the company. Any money which is given to the trust by the company must be used within nine months of the payment either to buy shares, repay borrowings or pay expenses. If these rules are met, the payments made by the company can be deducted for corporation tax purposes. The employees buy their shares from the trustees (the purchase money either being used to pay borrowings or to create a fund for future investment) and the trustees give the employee who buys an agreement that when it comes to selling, they will, if required, buy the shares back at the then current price. That way the trustees act as 'market makers', enabling employee shareholders to avoid being 'locked in' to the company and unable to sell their shares. The schemes are often used where a retiring employer wishes to enable his workforce to take over where it has no substantial funds available. In that case the employer would fund the trustees initially and employees could buy up shares as and when they could afford to do so. A time limit is imposed; shares acquired by the trustees must be disposed of within seven years. In such a scheme professional advice is again essential. Once established the workforce have to be told of the scheme (Letter 90).

Letter 90

Letter explaining an ESOP

As you will all know, my wife and I own all the shares in the Company. I am looking forward to being able to retire in a few years time and I have been taking advice as to ways in which I can make it possible for you all to take over from me when that day comes.

I realise that most of you do not have access to the large amount of capital that would be required and I would want to make it possible for all of you to have an opportunity to take a share rather than let the fortunate ones amongst you alone have the only chance.

I have been advised to establish an employee share ownership plan. What this means is that the Company will form a trust into which it will pay a substantial capital sum. All employees who have been with the Company for more than five years will be invited to become part of the trust and to nominate from amongst themselves two trustees. There will be one other trustee, Mr Stephen Robinson, the Company's solicitor. The trust will purchase shares from me and will offer those shares to you all. The purchase price which will be paid is the price which the auditors agree with the share valuation division of the Inland Revenue as the current market value of the shares. Every year, the Company will, from its profits, make further money available to the trustees and every year the trustees will buy shares from me and my wife at the market value and sell them to those of you who wish to buy. Ultimately, I hope that in this way, you will all have bought the Company between you.

I am altering the Articles of Association of the Company so as to remove the article that says that shares can only be transferred to me or my family and also the article that gives me the preferential right to any new shares. A new article will be inserted which will make it clear that if any employee leaves the company, he or she must sell back the shares he or she purchased under the trust.

The trust deed will provide that the trustees will, on request, repurchase shares, or find another employee to purchase them. The purchase price will be at the then market value of the shares.

I hope that this somewhat complicated machinery is understood by you all, but if you have any doubts or questions, I would be happy to try to answer them.

CHAPTER 9

Insolvency and death

9.1 Insolvency

When a company becomes insolvent it may suffer one of two different consequences. Any of its creditors who have security, that means some form of mortgage (in company terms a debenture is another word for mortgage), can appoint a receiver. The company continues to exist, its employees are not automatically dismissed and the receiver steps in and takes the place of the board of directors whose powers are suspended so long as the receivership continues. The receiver's duty is to receive the income of the company and pay it over to the creditor who appointed him or her. It is most likely that the receiver has been appointed 'receiver and manager'. That means that over and above the duty to collect in the money owing to the company and pay it out to the creditor, he/she has the task of managing the company and, if possible, trading with it so as to earn more money for the creditor. In that case the receiver will want to keep the workforce going and producing products which can be sold to help repay the debt. The receiver is not personally liable to pay the wages but has the duty to pay preferential debts of the company out of moneys that come into his/her hands. Wages are, amongst other special debts, preferential. So the receiver may not be personally liable but must see that the wages are paid before any ordinary creditor. If the receiver were to enter into a new contract with the employees, then he/she would make him-/herself personally liable. No receiver would do that. If there is no prospect of the company obtaining further business, the receiver should dismiss the workforce. Here is a case where the provisions of the Employment Protection Act against unfair dismissal have no application. The dismissal notice should indicate that the reason for dismissal is that the company is ceasing to carry on the business for which the employee was engaged. This is a prerequisite for a redundancy claim by the employee. Where, for example, the receiver decided to sell the company as a going concern, if the employees were dismissed and the business then sold as a going concern to some purchaser the employee's claim could be lost (*Secretary of State for Employment v. Spence* 1986 IRLR 248) (Letter 91).

Letter 91

Dismissal on insolvency

The Company has been unable to pay its debts and I have been appointed receiver by Newtown Bank PLC. The Company has ceased to trade and accordingly I hereby give you notice that your employment with the Company is terminated forthwith.

Any claim that you may have for unpaid wages or accrued holiday pay should be notified to me in writing and if agreed will be treated as a preferential debt.

Where no receiver is appointed, the other possibility is that the company will be wound up. Winding up (or liquidation – both expressions have virtually the same meaning in insolvency law) can take one of three forms. Where a company anticipates that it will within twelve months of the resolution to wind up be able to pay its debts in full, the shareholders can resolve on a 'members' voluntary winding up'. That means that the company is not insolvent, the shareholders decide who will be the liquidator and many problems may be avoided. Because of the now serious risks that directors and others run if they continue to trade when they 'knew or ought to have concluded that there was no reasonable prospect that the company would avoid going into insolvent liquidation', any director who can see that his or her company is solvent and can pay all its debts, but that if they go on much longer this will change and insolvency will follow, will if he or she is wise, cease to trade and recommend the shareholders to wind up voluntarily. On a decision to cease to trade, there is no automatic consequence for the employees. At that point, though, the question arises, 'do we give all employees notice or do we cease to trade but keep the workforce together and try to sell the business as a going concern?' If the decision is to try to sell then the overheads must be kept to a minimum. In Section 6.7 the point was made that there is no right, in the absence of a specific contract term, to lay off workers without pay. Where there is trade union representation in the company, the Employment Protection Act 1975 places an overriding duty on the employer when he or she proposes to dismiss employees as redundant to begin consultation with the recognised trade union at the earliest time. The choices are then to suspend the employees on full pay, attempt to obtain their agreement to accept lay off on terms that are less than full pay or to make them redundant on the grounds that the trade has ceased. In any event the union, if it is represented, should be consulted (Letter 92).

Letter 92

Letter consulting with trade union

Dear

It is with very real sadness that I have to tell you that as a result of the very serious downturn in trade we have been forced to decide to cease trading. We are contemplating making the workforce redundant and seek to find some purchaser for the goodwill and assets of the business.

The purpose of this letter is to inform you of the position so that you may consider the interests of your members and invite you to meet me so that we may consider together what can be done for the best.

We are proud of our workforce and would expect that if we could find a purchaser willing to acquire the business and inject the further capital that we lack, the purchaser might be willing to keep them together. We cannot afford to lay the workforce off with full pay. We might contemplate, as an alternative to immediate redundancy, lay off without pay for a period whilst a purchaser is sought.

This is of course a matter for discussion between us.

Yours sincerely

Where there is no alternative but to wind up, then the directors must cease trading, call a shareholders' meeting to resolve upon creditors winding up, call a meeting of creditors and accept that a liquidator be appointed. A liquidator is different from a receiver. In the first place, the appointment of a receiver does not bring the company's life to an end. The appointment of a liquidator does. The appointment of a receiver does not dismiss employees. The appointment of a liquidator does. The appointment of a receiver leaves the shareholders with rights and powers; the appointment of a liquidator replaces all the rights of the shareholders. Frequently, the appointment of a receiver will mean that the company goes into liquidation, so that there is both a receiver and a liquidator. In such a case, the receiver is the one who has possession of the assets of the business and until or or she has taken all he/she wants for the appointing creditor, the liquidator has no real function. Whether liquidator or receiver, though, preferential debts (which include the payment to the Revenue of PAYE deductions; national insurance contributions for the employees; contributions to any occupational pension scheme and unpaid wages and accrued holiday pay) must be paid out of the assets of the company in priority to any other creditor. Again, the first step of the liquidator, if the directors have not already taken it, will be to end all employment contracts. There is a distinction to be drawn between a liquidator who has been appointed by the Court on a compulsory winding up and a liquidator appointed by shareholders or creditors on a voluntary winding up. ('Shareholders' winding up' is the expression used in the case of a voluntary winding up of a solvent company; 'creditors' voluntary winding up' is also technically a winding up by the shareholders but in that case it is of an insolvent company; 'compulsory winding up' is the expression used when, following a petition to the Court, the Court orders that the company be wound up.) On a compulsory winding up, the employees are automatically dismissed, so the liquidator need do nothing except call for claims. In the case of voluntary winding up, a liquidator should give notice of immediate dismissal (Letter 93).

Letter 93

John Smith Limited (in liquidation)

TO ALL EMPLOYEES

The shareholders of the Company have resolved that by reason of its insolvency the Company must be wound up and I have been appointed by the creditors as the liquidator.

I give you notice that your employment by the Company is terminated forthwith. My assistant is on the premises securing them against entry by all persons. Any property that you claim to be your own should be identified to him together with proof of ownership if he calls for it. Only property that he agrees to release may be removed from the premises.

Any claim that you may have for unpaid wages or accrued holiday pay should be notified to me in writing and if agreed will be treated as a preferential debt. If you have any other claims against the Company you should inform me and a form for proof of debt will be sent to you.

A. Bloggs FCA
Liquidator

Where the employer is not a company, then the problem of involvency will be not the appointment of a receiver (it is possible for a receiver to be appointed but less usual) but an order of bankruptcy and the appointment of a trustee in bankruptcy. That does not automatically end the employment. Notice should be given just as in the case of a liquidator. Special provision has been made in the case of an apprentice or articled clerk. It is not common nowadays for a premium to be paid to a master to take an apprentice or an articled clerk. There is a problem for the apprentice or clerk who needs to complete his or her time. The trustee has power under the Insolvency Act to terminate the contract with the apprentice or clerk and to repay all or part of any premium paid. The trustee also has the power not to end the contract but to transfer it to someone else. The apprentice may not know of his/her rights so in fairness the trustee (or perhaps even the bankrupt employer) should write to the apprentice and let him/her know (Letter 94).

Letter 94

Letter to apprentice or articled clerk

Dear

I have been appointed the trustee in bankruptcy of Mr Jones, to whom you were articled. I do not want you to suffer because of Mr Jones' business failure and if you can find another solicitor who would take a transfer of your articles, I will be willing to execute such a transfer.

If you are uncertain to whom you could apply, may I suggest that you approach the Law Society for guidance.

Yours sincerely

9.2 Death

It is obvious that the death of an employee ends the contract of employment. Only if the employer is an individual (such as was discussed in the case of bankruptcy) would death bring the employment to an end. Many small businesspeople who trade as a limited company regard themselves and the company as one entity. They are not. A company is a completely separate entity in its own right and the 'owner' director is, him- or herself, only an employee of the company. Where an individual dies his or her business interests survive. It is for the businessperson's personal representative to make whatever arrangements have to be made to wind up his/her affairs. Where there is a will, things are easier. The only person who has the right to take action is the properly appointed personal representative. The expression 'personal representative' covers both an executor (who is appointed by a will) and an administrator (who is appointed by the Court where there is no will). The greatest difference comes from the fact that an executor gets all his or her powers from the will. This means that as soon as the death occurs, the executor has power to act. The expression 'proving the will' means exactly that – does the Will exist?; then prove it. There is only one way to prove that it exists, and that is by an application for what is called 'probate'. Technically, probate is an order of the court proving that a will exists and that the person named as executor is the executor. The risk that one takes in acting before the grant has been made is that another will might be found and that you are not the executor. In that case you could have a liability for anything that you have done. If you are confident and urgent action is required, then proceed. Where a business is involved decisions cannot be put off until a grant of probate has been made. The obvious first problem is to see that there is someone ready and willing to carry on the business in the meantime. That someone, more likely than not, is the existing manager. Write to the manager (Letter 95).

Letter 95

Letter from an executor authorising a manager to continue to act

Dear

I am executor of Fred Thompson's will. I have yet to get everything sorted out and in the meantime I do hope that you will continue the excellent work that you have been doing since Fred's death in keeping the business running.

I will make arrangements with the bank to give you a limited power of cheque signing. I think that your signature alone for amounts less than £500 and my signature for sums in excess of that would meet the case. If this creates problems let me know.

So far as your position is concerned, this letter confirms that your employment continues under the terms of your contract of employment with Fred. Tell all the others that I am writing to them in similar terms.

I have my responsibilities to the beneficiaries under the will so will you please arrange to be at the works at 4 p.m. next Wednesday so that I can go through the current order book and accounts and see what is the up-to-date position. Could you also give instructions to the bookkeeper that I will need to have a monthly income and expenditure statement and a list of outstanding debts and creditors. In each case I shall want to know how long the debt or credit has existed.

The auditors will be contacting you to make arrangements to prepare accounts as at the date of Fred's death.

If there are any problems or questions please let me know.

Again I give you the thanks of the family as well as my own for your help in this sad time.

Yours sincerely

As indicated in Letter 95 it is necessary to write to all the employees to confirm to them that their contracts of employment are being continued. Quite apart from any legal consideration, they will be concerned to know their position. They will know that their 'boss' has died and will wonder whether their jobs are safe. Confirm the position to them. If there are many employees a note in the wage packet might be appropriate. If there are only a few (as would be more probable in the situation we are considering), then write individually. Letter 96 would be appropriate.

Letter 96

Letter to employees on death of sole trader

Dear

I am the executor of Fred Thompson's will and am responsible for organising his affairs for the family.

I want you all to know that the family intend to see that, despite Fred's death, the business will continue. So far as you are concerned, your employment contract will be unaffected and, following from Fred's death, I as executor will take responsibility until the will has been proved and a further decision can be taken for the future.

Until then, I have asked Mr Smith to carry on as Manager. I will try to keep you informed about future plans but, as you will probably realise, it will be some months before the estate can be fully administered and things brought back to normal.

Yours sincerely

Where there is no will a problem exists. The sort of things that will have to be done are illustrated by Letter 93. If there is no will there is no one to take action. The widow or widower, as the case may be, will be first on the list of possible applicants. If there is no widow or widower, then the children have equal rights. The family problems that can arise if one child goes ahead without consultation with his or her siblings can be imagined. There is no choice but for a family meeting to decide who is going to apply. Even then it is quite unsafe to act without the grant of Letter of Administration. Once the grant has been made (and even with the most efficient of advisers this can take time), then action can be taken. With no will as guidance, family agreement will be needed to decide what is to be done with the business. Maybe one or other of the family will take it over. Before that happens, the employees technically have no contract of employment. The death of the employer ended their contract and who is going to give them a replacement? One member of the family must take the initiative. Write Letter 97.

Letter 97

Letter to manager on death of employer

Dear

I am sorry to say that my father died without making a will. As you can imagine, this does complicate things considerably. I am trying to sort out his affairs and one or other of us will be applying for a grant of Letters of Administration to his estate. Meantime, I would be grateful if you would continue running the business as you are at the moment. I have no authority to take formal action but I will be seeing the bank this afternoon to see what arrangements can be made as a temporary measure to keep things going.

I am sure that my brothers and sisters will want to see that the business continues under your leadership but, as I say, until a grant of Letters of Administration has been made, neither I nor anyone else has any power to make a decision.

Thank you for all that you are doing.

Yours sincerely

9.3 Death of an employee in service

As mentioned, on the death of an employee his or her contract automatically ends. The employer will have to account to the estate for any unpaid wages or accrued holiday pay and provide the details of pay and tax to date of death so that any tax repayment claim can be made. If the employee was a member of the company's pension scheme then his or her family must be told so that they can make any claim and the trustees (or insurers) of the scheme must be informed. Write Letter 98 to the family and Letter 99 to the pension fund.

Letter 98

Letter to family of deceased employee

Dear Mrs

May I say how sad we all are to learn of the death of your husband. He has always been most highly regarded by us all and amongst his fellow workers was popular and well loved. He will be sadly missed.

I enclose herewith a cheque for £   which represents the pay and unpaid holiday to the date of his death. I also enclose the tax form recording the pay and tax position in case there is any tax refund due to him.

I do not know whether he explained to you that he was a member of the Company's pension scheme. Under this scheme there are moneys due to you. I am afraid that I cannot tell you what the figures are and I have written to the trustees of the fund asking them to contact you direct. They will certainly need a copy of the death certificate and, possibly, also a copy of your marriage certificate.

If you have any problems or need any help to manage Fred's affairs, please do not hesitate to get in touch with me. If you need legal help, I am sure that the Company's lawyers will assist. Let me know if you would like me to do so and I will put you in touch with them.

Again, may I offer my sympathy to you and your family at this sad time.

Yours sincerely

Personnel Manager

Letter 99

Letter to pension trustees

Dear

Conglomerates Ltd pension scheme

I regret to have to inform you of the death of Frederick Thompson, a member of the Company's pension scheme. He was aged 63 and had forty years of service with the Company. His wage at the time of his death was £15,000 per annum.

I believe that under the scheme he is entitled to the death in service benefit of a lump sum, return of contributions and a death grant. Perhaps you could confirm the position to me. I have written to the widow, Mrs Rosalind Thompson, whose address is The Gables, 24 Pendragon Road, Hollingsworth, Leicestershire, and I have told her that you will be in contact with her and I have warned her that you will probably require to see the death certificate and her marriage certificate.

Yours faithfully

Personnel Manager

Appendix A: Code of discipline and disciplinary procedure

Code of discipline

1. Aims

(a) The purpose of the Code is to provide:
  (i) a sound basis for the maintenance of discipline within the organisation;
  (ii) a clear understanding between the management and the employees of the need for discipline; and
  (iii) a mutually acceptable procedure for dealing with any breaches of discipline.

(b) A disciplinary Code is necessary for the fair treatment of all employees and the following rules (in conjunction with the discipline procedure) set standards of performance and behaviour at work.

(c) The rules are designed to promote fairness and order in the treatment of individuals within the organisation.

(d) The procedure seeks to ensure that satisfactory standards are maintained and provides a fair method of dealing with any shortcomings in the form of breaches of contract.

2. Principles

(a) **An important aim of this Code is to encourage the employee whose conduct or standard of work performance is unsatisfactory to remedy the situation**.
The procedure is designed to work as quickly as possible, consistent with thorough investigations of the facts at each stage.

(b) The employee will be made aware of any shortcomings and will be given the opportunity to present an explanation before any decision as to disciplinary action is taken.

(c) The employee must always be informed in writing of any disciplinary action taken and the reason for it.

(d) The employee's trade union representative (where recognition is applicable) will be informed when a written warning is issued and will be given a copy of the notification if the employee so wishes.

(e) An employee who has received written notification of any disciplinary action will acknowledge receipt by his or her signature on the copy of the notice.

(f) An employee will have the right, at any stage of the disciplinary procedure, to appeal to a higher level of management.

(g) The employee will have the right, at any stage of the disciplinary procedure, to be represented by a trade union representative (if trade union recognition is applicable) or by a person of his or her choice.

(h) The level that is authorised to impose each form of disciplinary action will be clearly known to management and the employees.

(i) These rules outline the essential features of a fair and reasonable disciplinary procedure indicating that:

  (i) discipline need not always be punitive;

  (ii) it is also meant to teach and to corrrect, etc;

  (iii) before any action is taken, the matter should be thoroughly investigated;

  (iv) the employee at all times should be made aware of the cause for complaint, and given the opportunity to present a fair defence and explanation of the matter complained of;

  (v) the rights of appeal and representation at all stages of the procedure are guaranteed.

3. Time limits

Disciplinary action will be undertaken as promptly as possible at all stages, and in normal circumstances within   days.

4. Listing of offences

While it is not possible to list all the offences or to specify the nature of the disciplinary action in each case, every offence will be carefully considered and disciplinary action taken according to the gravity of the offence.

5. Gross misconduct

Types of offences which constitute gross misconduct, which – it should be noted – is open-ended, are outlined in the disciplinary procedure. If sufficient grounds are thought to exist that give the employer a reasonable belief in the guilt of the employee, then the summary dismissal of the employee will follow. The normal rules of investigation and representation will be observed, and it may be that the employee would be suspended on or off pay for   hours prior to the summary dismissal. In the event that summary dismissal is the sanction taken against the employee concerned, then the entitlement to notice as specified by the Employment Protection (Consolidation) Act 1978 will not apply, and the employer reserves the right to impose SUMMARY DISMISSAL as the sanction.

6. Unsatisfactory conduct

Examples of unsatisfactory conduct are detailed in the discipline procedure – it should be noted that this list is open-ended. In the event that sufficient grounds exist for the termination of the employee's contract of employment for reasons of unsatisfactory conduct, then the employee will be interviewed by the appropriate authority, and the rules regarding representation and appeals will apply.

The decision as to whether or not the employee stands to be dismissed will rest with the employer, but only after a reasonable belief has been established by the employer that the employee's unsatisfactory conduct has become such as to merit the dismissal. Notice may be waived in such cases but payment in lieu of notice would then apply.

7. The disciplinary procedure

General matters

It is recognised that discipline is essential for the successful conduct of the undertaking's business, and for the safety and the well-being of all the employees. In accepting this, it is equally recognised that, if appropriate, disciplinary action should be considered and applied fairly and equitably. Within the limitations of delegated managerial responsibility, the appropriate level of management shall have the right to dismiss, suspend with or without pay or demote the employee concerned – subject to the right of appeal being exercised by the employee faced with punitive measures for his or her breach of the employment contract – always ensuring that the procedure is strictly adhered to.

8. Summary suspension or dismissal

Employees will not normally be dismissed for a FIRST OFFENCE, but there are certain cases of GROSS MISCONDUCT which are likely to lead to the employee being SUMMARILY DISMISSED without any prior warnings – oral or written.

9. Gross misconduct

The following are examples of GROSS MISCONDUCT which, it should be noted, could result in instant dismissal:

(a) serious offences against the interests of the undertaking – including wilful injury to others and wilful damage to property that belongs to the undertaking or where the undertaking has an interest;
(b) incapacity during working hours due to the effect of alcohol or drugs;
(c) fraudulent wage/salary claims – including the falsification of time-sheets and other material matters that affect the payment of wages or salary;
(d) gross insubordination;
(e) failure to obey critical SAFETY RULES, e.g. smoking in a NO-SMOKING area;
(f) fighting in the workplace or anywhere on the undertaking's premises or areas wherein the undertaking has an interest;
(g) alleged theft from the employer or any employee connected with the undertaking – provided that the allegation is established as fact to the reasonable belief of the employer;
(h) theft from any member of the public, if the work done by the employee brings that employee into contact with the public;
(i) false particulars that are given by the employee when applying for the job being done – any mis-statement on the application form would be viewed as a potential breach of trust and would raise serious questions as to the potential loyalty of the individual concerned – no matter what the reason for the mis-statement;
(j) criminal convictions that would have a material bearing on the employee's work – the Statute of Limitations is observed by the undertaking.

THIS LIST IS NOT EXHAUSTIVE.

No decision on gross misconduct will be taken until the employee has been interviewed – if applicable, in the presence of his or her trade union official – or accompanied by another person of his or her choice. A full explanation by the employee will be judged on its merits and weighed against the reasonable belief of the employer after all the circumstances have been investigated.

Consideration will be given to any mitigating circumstances that might be offered. A lesser penalty may be imposed which may take the form of SUSPENSION WITHOUT PAY and a FINAL WARNING instead of dismissal – provided that the employee concerned agrees to such punitive measures. In any event, the decision will be confirmed in writing together with the clear reasons for the action taken – Statement of reasons for . . ..

10. Records

Where an offence warrants summary dismissal but the employer has – due to mitigating circumstances – imposed a lesser penalty, which would include a FINAL WRITTEN WARNING, then this will be noted and, where appropriate, will remain permanently on the employee's record card.

11. Unsatisfactory conduct (other than Gross Misconduct)

Instances of any failure to observe and maintain departmental discipline, which are less serious than offences constituting Gross Misconduct, are termed Unsatisfactory Conduct and will lead to warnings (both verbal and written) and/or punitive measures being taken that are short of dismissal. Offences under this heading – which, it should be noted would be within the reasonable belief of the employer – include:

(a) bad time-keeping;
(b) absence from work without a reasonable cause – this includes the requirement that an employee should notify the employer as to ill-health by NOON on the first day of illness;
(c) an unacceptable standard of work performance, general application to the work required to be done, a lack of capability to do the work after training and guidance;
(d) general negligence at work;
(e) refusal to carry out a reasonable instruction or order given by an accredited authority within the undertaking.

THIS LIST IS NOT EXHAUSTIVE.

12. An oral or a written warning

(a) Where an employee's work is such as to warrant admonition, the appropriate authority within the undertaking shall give a warning to the employee, which shall be confirmed in writing. The employee should be left in no doubt about the reason and the grounds for the warning, and should be advised of the potential consequences of any repetition of the conduct.

(b) Warnings should be explicit and should indicate what standards of performance and conduct are expected, the ways in which an employee falls short of the expected standards, what should be done to rectify the situation and what sanctions will be imposed if the employee fails – within a reasonable period of time – to rectify the situation.

(c) A written record of warnings must be kept and the employee so informed. The further omission or commission of a similar act, or subsequent but different offence, may result in either punitive disciplinary action or in a further warning – which might be a FINAL WARNING.

13. Final warning

Written notification of a FINAL WARNING will specify that any repetition of the offence, or a committal of any other serious offence within a period of twelve months or any other period that may be required by the undertaking, will result in dismissal being considered as the only option open to the employer. Where appropriate, should a trade union recognition agreement apply, then a copy of the warning will be given to the trade union representative for the record.

14. Record of warnings

In the event that disciplinary action has had to be taken for the reason that the employee has committed a breach of the rules – bad time-keeping, unauthorised absenteeism or other failure to maintain acceptable standards of conduct or performance – the employee should complete a consecutive period of   of satisfactory conduct. Should that be the case, then the employee's relevant warning will be removed from the record and the employee considered to have made a fresh start.

15. Final Warning – effective record of

A FINAL WRITTEN WARNING of dismissal from the employment will remain in force until the employee has completed a period of satisfactory conduct – from the date of the offence. The entry of the FINAL WARNING will then be expunged from the employee's record except in serious cases that will remain within the employer's discretion.

16. Appeal against oral or written warnings

Appeals against oral or written warnings may be made to the appropriate authority within the undertaking. Within a two-week period following the notification of the appeal, the employee – accompanied by his or her trade union representative – if a recognition agreement applies – or by another person of the employee's choice, will be interviewed by the appropriate authority within the undertaking and given an adequate opportunity to offer an explanation for the offence alleged. The appropriate authority within the undertaking must not have had any direct connection with the circumstances that led up to the imposition of the disciplinary action.

17. Suspension with pay

The appropriate authority within the undertaking shall have the necessary delegated powers to SUSPEND an employee who is considered to be creating a situation where there is a danger to that particular employee or other employees, or where the management consider it to be necessary to remove the employee from the place of work in order to conduct an investigation into all the relevant circumstances surrounding a potentially serious alleged breach of the employment contract. Such a suspension is not disciplinary action – although it might be that subsequent matters will come to light that may lead to disciplinary action being taken.

Any employee who is so suspended shall have the suspension confirmed in writing within two days of the suspension taking place. In the event that the suspension with pay lasts for more than two weeks, then the employee shall have the right to seek – in writing – the reasons for his or her continued suspension. This shall be provided by the appropriate authority.

Suspension on full pay does not exclude the possibility that punitive disciplinary action will be taken after a full investigation. In any circumstances which involve or may involve criminal proceedings against the employee, there is no need for the suspension to continue until the outcome of the said criminal proceedings is known. In such cases, dependent upon the reasonable belief of the employer in the matters that have led to the criminal proceedings being taken, then the employer may take the appropriate disciplinary action. This must depend upon the REASONABLE BELIEF of the employer and not just on an assumption of the employee's guilt.

18. Appeals against final warnings or punitive disciplinary action and dismissal

When an employee has received a FINAL WRITTEN WARNING or has been summarily dismissed or suspended without pay, or where an employee has been advised that dismissal will take effect from a future date, then the employee shall be notified – in writing – of the reason for the proposed action, and if the employee considers that a dismissal, or a suspension with loss of earnings is, or would be unfair, an appeal may be lodged – in writing – to the appropriate authority within the undertaking. If there is a trade union recognition agreement currently subsisting, then the appeal may be undertaken by the representative of the employee. The appeal must be lodged within two weeks of the notification of the action being received by the employee.

Appeals shall be heard promptly, normally not later than one month after lodgement unless there are exceptional circumstances. The authority hearing the appeal shall have had no connection with the matters that led to the disciplinary measures being taken. It shall have the delegated power of the undertaking to decide the appeal.

19. Procedure for the consideration of the appeal

Notice of the appeal date shall be given to the appellant at least SEVEN DAYS before the date of the hearing. The appellant may be represented – should a recognition agreement with a trade union subsist – by his or her representative, or by a person of his or her choice.

The following procedure shall be adopted at the appeal:

(a) The management representative shall have the opportunity to ask questions of the appellant and/or the appellant's representative, and of any witnesses called by the appellant.

(b) The appellant and/or the appellant's representative shall put the appellant's case in the presence of the management representative.

(c) The management representative shall put the undertaking's case in the presence of the appellant and the appellant's representative.

(d) The appellant and/or the appellant's representative shall have the opportunity to ask questions of the management's representative and any witnesses called by the management.

(e) The members of the undertaking who comprise the Appeals Committee shall have the opportunity to ask questions of either party, and of any witnesses appearing on behalf of either party.

(f) The management representative, and thereafter the appellant and/or the appellant's representative, shall have the opportunity – if they so wish – to sum up their case but not introducing any new material unless the Appeals Committee allow such new material – which may then result in the appeal being adjourned in order that the new material may be looked at in detail.

(g) The management representative, the appellant, the appellant's representative and any witnesses shall than withdraw. The Appeals Committee shall deliberate in private. It shall have the ability to recall either party to the appeal in order that clarification of any particular points that have arisen in the evidence may be sought. If a recall is necessary, then both parties should be present, notwithstanding only one party is concerned with the point that has given rise to the recall.

The Appeals Committee shall announce its decision in one of the following ways:

(i) that the grounds for the appeal have been substantiated and that the appeal is upheld;

(ii) that the grounds for the appeal have been substantiated in part and that the appeal is upheld to the extent that a lesser form of punitive action is recommended;

(iii) that the grounds for the appeal have not been substantiated and that the appeal is therefore dismissed.

The grievance procedure

The procedure for the settlement of grievances and disputes

To ensure that any grievances relating to employment are settled fairly, speedily and as near to the point of origin as possible, the following procedure shall be adhered to should a grievance arise.

(a) Stage 1
Any employee or group of employees feeling aggrieved on any matter, excepting those that that fall within the disciplinary procedure, should discuss the matter with the designated authority within the undertaking who is in direct control of that particular part of the undertaking.

(b) Action by the designated authority
The designated authority shall discuss the nature of the grievance with
the employee or group of employees and thereafter, where appropriate
(trade union recognition agreement applies), with the trade union
representative. If the designated authority feels unable to accept the
legitimacy of the grievance, or a remedy cannot be provided, then the
authority shall reply to the aggrieved party/parties within two working
days and advise orally of the next step in the procedure.

(c) Stage 2
If the employee or a group of employees is dissatisfied with the reply,
the matter should be put in writing – indicating the nature of the
grievance – it should be sent to the senior management of the
undertaking within five working days. The senior management shall
hear the grievance in the presence of the aggrieved employee or
employees together – and, where appropriate – the trade union
representative (provided that a recognition agreement subsists).

(d) Action by the senior management
After having fully investigated the circumstances surrounding the
grievance, the senior management of the undertaking shall reply in
writing to the complaint as soon as possible, and in any case within five
working days, giving the reasons for the decision that has been taken.

(e) Stage 3
If the issues that are complained of are not resolved after this stage of
the procedure, then the employee/employees – or, where there subsists
a recognition agreement, the trade union official – shall write to the
employer and seek his or her agreement to take the matter complained
of to ACAS (The Advisory, Conciliation and Arbitration Service) for its
independent assessment.

Health safety complaints

In the event that matters are complained of that relate to the health,
safety and welfare of the undertaking and the employees therein, then
the procedure is as follows:

(a) Stage 1
Where a Safety Committee is functioning (usually only in the circumstance of a trade union recognition agreement subsisting), then the
complaint is referred to that Committee in line with the current Safety
Policy as operated by the undertaking.

(b) Stage 2

In the event that there is no Safety Committee recognised by the undertaking, then the complaint shall be heard in the first instance by the immediate supervisor of the area and employees where the complaint had arisen. In the event that the matter cannot be dealt with as soon as is reasonably practicable, then the matter must be referred to the highest level within the undertaking – if a hazard or immediate danger to the employees is apparent, then the area should be cleared and the appropriate action taken.

Addendum

THE FOLLOWING SHOULD BE NOTED BY ALL EMPLOYEES:
Under no circumstances will complaints that purport to be founded on matters concerning the health and safety of the undertaking, which after sufficient investigation are established as ill-founded and within the reasonable belief of the employer to be malicious mis-use of the Safety Policy of the undertaking, be in any way tolerated. Any employee or group of employees making such complaints will be subject to the disciplinary procedure and will be looked upon as being guilty of gross misconduct.

It may be that complaints are made that touch upon the health and safety of the undertaking, and that such complaints are – in part – justified. The complainant will have his or her complaint looked into, and if it is within the reasonable belief of the employer that malicious intent is not a motive, but that a genuine grievance is behind the complaint, then, although disciplinary action might be an option, the benefit of the doubt shall be given to the complainant.

Appendix B: Trade union recognition agreement

THIS IS AN AGREEMENT MADE BETWEEN THE PARTIES NAMED HEREUNDER AS TO THE REGULATION AND CONTROL OF THE TERMS AND CONDITIONS OF EMPLOYMENT OF THE MEMBERS EMPLOYED BY BLOGGS & CO.

The parties to this agreement are:

The Employer   Blogg & Co.

The Trade Union   The Union of

Wherein it is agreed that the following terms and conditions shall apply to all the members of the union in the employ of Bloggs & Co and that this agreement shall subsist until such time as this agreement be either terminated by due notice by either party, or until such amendment as may be necessary be added, or until such time as material events require that this agreement be re-negotiated by the parties.

1. It is agreed that all employees of Bloggs & Co will, if they so wish, be permitted to join the union.
2. It is agreed that all new entrants to Bloggs & Co's employ will be informed of their right to join the union if they so wish.
3. The wages and salaries paid to employees of Bloggs & Co will be by agreement with the union and the employer and will be the going rate for the job.
4. The holiday and public holiday entitlements for all employee members will be by agreement with the union.
5. Overtime will be a matter for negotiation between Blogg & Co and the union.
6. Disciplinary and grievance procedures will include a clause that gives the elected shop steward within the workplace the right to represent members who may be subject to the disciplinary rules of the Company or who may wish to avail themselves of the grievance procedure on some matter or other.

7. The elected and accredited shop steward will be granted reason-
    able time off so as to attend courses and seminars and other union
    meetings that are directly associated with Bloggs & Co's industrial
    relations policy. The elected and appointed safety representative
    shall be granted reasonable time off so as to improve his or her
    knowledge of the Health and Safety at Work Act and the
    accompanying Regulations, so that he or she may perform the
    duties of a safety representative efficiently and as per the policy of
    the union and the Health and Safety Commission. In both cases
    the time off shall be with pay – earnings as would be achieved
    during the course of ordinary working practice – and shall include
    any overtime/bonus earnings that might apply whilst the repres-
    entative is off on union duties.

8. Bonus payments relating to work and systems of work as operated
    by Bloggs & Co shall be paid to all members of the union by
    agreement with the union or the union's elected shop steward
    acting on the mandate of the members.

9. The union agrees to assist the employer in the enforcement of any
    legally enforceable regulations that cover the health and safety at
    work of its members, and to ensure that the members co-operate
    at all times in these matters.

10. In the event of a failure to agree in matters concerning industrial
    relations within Bloggs & Co's employment, the union and the
    employer agree that the assistance of ACAS shall be sought in
    order that a quick resolvement to the disputed matters is effected.

11. In the event that industrial action is undertaken by the members
    before mediation and conciliation is undertaken, then the union
    will do all that is practicable so as to seek a resolvement to the
    action and facilitation of return to work so that normal negoti-
    ations may be undertaken.

12. In the event that a shop steward or a safety representative stands
    to be disciplined by Bloggs & Co under the disciplinary pro-
    cedure, then it is agreed that a full-time official of the union will
    be called in so as to oversee that the action required to be taken
    by the employer is fair and reasonable.

13. Redundancy matters will be governed by the 'last in first out'
    principle of selection, with the exception of agreed areas of skill
    that will allow a limited form of selection of employees for a
    pending redundancy.

14. Should matters concerning redundancy be forecast by the Com-
    pany, then it is incumbent upon the Company to inform the union
    as soon as is reasonable so that negotiations be undertaken that
    can minimise the problem as it affects the membership.

No-strike clause (often incorporated in modern trade union agreements)

15.   The union undertakes to prevent industrial action taking place within Bloggs & Co until all avenues open to the union are fully explored with a view to the settlement of the particular dispute. The union will undertake to require the members to attend work throughout all the stages of negotiation, and will utilise the provisions of the union rule book and this Agreement in order that the members follow the union's advice. Should the members take industrial action in spite of the union's request then the union will treat the members' action as being outwith the terms of reference of this Agreement and the union's representation.

Should all attempts at a resolvement fail – which will include the services of ACAS and/or some other independent arbitration tribunal, the union may review its position, dependent upon the matters that are in dispute and the effect that these matters will or will not have on the membership of the union within Bloggs & Co.

THIS AGREEMENT SIGNED BY THE PARTIES:

FOR THE UNION

Bloggs & Co

Dated

Appendix C: The Health and Safety at Work Act 1974: advice notes, check lists, policies, occupational health brief

THESE NOTES INCLUDE A PREAMBLE AND CONCISE DETAILS AS TO PRECAUTIONS AND GOOD PRACTICE WITHIN THE UNITED KINGDOM AS RELATED TO THE STATUTORY LAW AND THE ATTENDANT REGULATIONS

General notes on health as related to employment

The inter-relationship of work and health has many facets, these include:

1. the recognition, evaluation and control of hazards in the working environment;
2. the early diagnosis of stress and strain suffered by employees through arduous duties and a complete commitment to their employment;
3. prevention of absence through ill-health;
4. the fitness of employees for their employment in the particular environment, early assessment at interview and decision as to employ;
5. rehabilitation (alcoholism, drugs, personal problems) action on such matters being considered with care and avoidance of dismissal where practicable;
6. the human factor related to accidents at work;
7. mental health and morale at work.

There are two main areas of inter-relationship between work and health, although any division between the two is by no means clear-cut:

(a) the effect of work on health;
(b) the effect of health on work.

The effect of work on health

This area concerns all those physical, chemical, biological and physiological factors at work which can affect the health of the employee. It therefore includes industrial diseases arising from the exposure to dusts, fumes, gas, and noise, etc., but it will also include the effect of automation, shift-work, job satisfaction and the environment. As health is the target to aim for it must be concerned with improving the working environment in order to avoid stress and fatigue. The highest possible standards that are practicable for the employer should be attained.

The responsibility for the achievement of high environmental standards must rest with the employer. The employer's attention to these matters and his or her awareness of the problems, his/her expectations of short-term gains, and his/her far sightedness should be demonstrated. At best, the employer will be far in advance of the general standard that is required under the Health and Safety at Work Act 1974 and the attendant regulations. At worst the employer will fall short of the general standard and this might well result not only in the business suffering through absenteeism and ill-health among the employees but also through the employer suffering from the imposed penalties that are available to the Health and Safety Executive under the Act.

This area of the effect of work on health is therefore dependent upon measures taken at the workplace to modify it in the interests of the workforce. It is believed that by so doing the worker will be better able to function, and that an advantage will accrue thereby to the employer and the community at large. There are of course statutory requirements relevant to the temperature, cleanliness, noise, dust and fumes within the workplace, and these are ignored at the peril of the employer. Better by far that the employer exceeds these standards in the running of the business.

Many small and middle-sized businesses will find it difficult through limitations on finance and motivation to establish maximum standards, but the attempt and the willingness of these employers to reach even half-way will, nevertheless, ensure that the accident rate will be reduced and the possible absenteeism of workers will be similarly reduced, so enabling the business to re-invest in the improvement of the standards that should be attained.

The effect of health on work

Any departure from the state of complete physical, mental and social well-being affects working capacity and, thereby, the employer's business stability and profitability. In its most obvious form the effect of health on work is seen from the annual figures for sickness absence which now exceeds the massive total of some 300,000,000 working days per annum. This may be compared with an average of some 300,000 days lost from industrial action, and it can be seen that the economic importance is obvious. To a lesser extent the problems inherent in the effect of health on work can be seen in long-term chronic illness, mental or physical, and the difficulties in rehabilitation that stem from them.

Almost entirely hidden from view are the health-related problems affecting people remaining at work, who, for one reason or another, individually or indeed collectively, are less fit than they should be. Responsibility for this area is less easy to assign. In one respect there is an individual responsibility as far as personal habits of smoking, drinking, eating and exercise are concerned in that these habits can undoubtedly undermine the person's ability to perform any function, and the control of them is up to the individual. In another respect there is community responsibility for clean air, water and food, for housing, town planning and social amenities, all of which promote and maintain high standards of personal health.

Morale, and the effect of stress and strain relative to work bring together the two areas and the border between the effect of health on work and of work on health now becomes blurred. The two sets of problems become inseparable. This is an area of mental health in which the individual plays a very personal role as he/she brings his/her private conflicts to work where adverse or favourable factors and influences that may alter the result make it difficult to disentangle the cause from the effect.

An employer who can maintain a stable and safe working environment will minimise his or her loss sustained through aggravated absence that has been caused by the adverse working conditions or working systems that the susceptible employee has been affected by. Simplistic examples are long periods in an uncomfortable posture, bad lighting, excessive heat or cold, undue pressure of work, ordinary every-day conditions encountered in many workplaces. None of these examples are easily corrected, but any one of them can be alleviated to some extent, with the subsequent cost of the correction being more than cancelled out by the improvement in the attendance levels of the employees.

A practical approach to risk control

The principle of risk control is to view the whole situation, identify the risks, evaluate such risks, and eliminate or control them. The elimination or control requires, in some instances, careful consideration of many aspects such as risks related to the probability of an occurrence, economics, the practicabilities or the desirability of eliminating hazard and the resultant cost to the organisation.

The following notes are EXAMPLES of the approach to risk control and should be used for the classification and identification of risks. Good working conditions for employees not only reduce the potential accident and fire hazards, but provide a better feeling of well-being for the employees, thereby resulting in the improvement of production and efficiency, and possibly an improved family and community relationship.

Factors in the environment

These can be considered as being divided into five groups:

(a) safety factors, e.g. the guarding of machinery and equipment;
(b) chemical factors, e.g. these include domestic aids and drugs;
(c) physical factors, e.g. strain at work through lifting or posture;
(d) ergonomic factors, e.g. all matters of stress and strain;
(e) welfare factors, e.g. good working conditions.

The basic approach

If the employer is to create and maintain safe working conditions, it is essential that some kind of basic and competent approach be utilised. That which is often used for general problem solving can be suitably adopted, and effectively this involves looking into the five separate stages. For example, regular meetings between management and supervisors, primarily or solely in order to discuss matters of health and safety welfare and conditions in general, in the same way as one would organise meetings to discuss problems of productivity.

SPECIAL NOTE: THESE DEFINITIONS WILL APPLY TO ANY TYPE OF EMPLOYMENT, FROM THAT CONCERNED WITH HEAVY INDUSTRY TO THE SMALL BUSINESS WITH VERY FEW EMPLOYEES.

The definitions for discussion headings are:

(a) measurement (cost/justification/risk factor);
(b) evaluation (judgement as to business benefit);
(c) control (decision taking by senior management);

(d) check (comprehensive checking of possible hazards);
(e) maintain (often forgotten or neglected).

Apply the logic of the above five stages to cope with the vast majority
of problems encountered in the day-to-day running of the business.

Example: chemical factors in the workplace (a first priority since October 1989)
Acids, alkalies, chemicals, compressed and liquified gases, solvents and
household detergents, all represent chemicals in the environment of the
workplace, and indeed in the home as well. Where there are any of
these present, problems are capable of arising and perhaps in three
phases:

(a) potential;
(b) actual;
(c) future.

Thus, flammable liquids present potential problems. Actual problems
occur when a harmful substance or reaction product of the substance
reaches a susceptible part of the body, e.g. ammonia will injure the
eyes; combustion products may create toxic gasses (burning furniture
with plastic or foam content).

   Knowing that chemicals have the potential to cause injury, there has
to be some insurance against the likelihood of that and only 'good
housekeeping' by the user in the provision of storage, movement, use
and disposal will cut the risk.

   It is suggested that the following will assist the employer to formulate
a plan:

(a) Identify: list all the chemicals and chemical products involved in
     the workplace. Gases, cleaners, acids and alkalies;
(b) Classify: separate into their related groups: GASES; ACIDS;
     CAUSTIC SODA; FLAMMABLE MATERIALS; CHLORIN-
     ATED SOLVENTS; POISONS; OILS AND PARAFFIN;
     PLASTICS; DOMESTIC BLEACH (AMMONIA) (when accid-
     ently mixed gives off phosgene gas), ammonia being readily used
     in office cleaning, and often used by untrained staff.

Define storage requirements

FLAMMABLE LIQUIDS MAY REQUIRE BRICK-BUILT
STORES OR STEEL LOCKERS, DEPENDING UPON THE
FLASH POINT AND THE QUANTITY. FLAME-PROOF LIGHT
FITTINGS MAY BE NEEDED. AMMONIA BOTTLES SHOULD
NOT BE STORED AGAINST OR NEAR HOT RADIATORS

(THEY OFTEN ARE IN OFFICES AND STOREROOMS). THE
GLASS BOTTLES CAN, AND DO EXPLODE. PROPER LABEL-
LING IS ABSOLUTELY IMPERATIVE.

Some final points to note

It is an executive managerial responsibility to provide safe and healthy
working conditions. Hygienists, safety advisers and other specialists can
provide proper guidance; they cannot implement the changes needed.
Previous factory law has been described as being good in some areas
and bad in others. It has been further suggested that the Health and
Safety at Work Act 1974 is like removing patchy whitewash from a wall
and redecorating it evenly. The Act was clearly designed to provide an
opportunity and a challenge to the making of a lot of improvements. It
uses the principle of accountability and not the principle of responsibility; however the combination of the Factory Act 1961, the Offices,
Shops and Railway Premises Act 1963, the various regulations and the
Codes of Practice clearly lays a high degree of both accountability and
responsibility on the employer, and to a lesser extent, the employee.

Responsibility is heavy stuff, so to meet at least some of the
requirements and to show by example that you are prepared to try and
conform to the legislation and improve your establishment and systems
of work, try the following:

Suggestions

(a) Start in a small way – one subject at a time.
(b) List all the problems that are apparent, i.e., a blocked fire exit.
(c) Classify all the hazards applicable to your workplace.
(d) Work out a corrective procedure – a better system of work control.
(e) Identify the resources needed – finance/administration.
(f) Institute the systems and the controls.
(g) Define the people responsible for, and those accountable for, safety.
(h) Plan to ensure that control standards are maintained.
(i) Do not attempt too much at one – correct by degree.
(j) Ensure that all the staff are aware of the Company's safety policy.
(k) Ensure that all the staff are aware of their own responsibilities
within the parameters of the health and safety legislation, and
beyond that basic boundary.

In-house training for safety and safe systems of work

Each personnel group, workplace and the organisation as a whole require to conform to the perfect safety function and must be covered adequately so as to ensure that all areas in the field of health, safety and welfare are involved, otherwise the recommended training may well be inadequate.

Taking each personnnel group within the Company, or any associated group, the following areas must be covered completely so as to ensure effective results and a safer environment. The October 1989 Regulations relating to the use and storage of the many chemical and chemically based substances in use in the majority of workplaces are a most important factor for all management and employers in general to note. The number of accidents, incidents involving chemicals leading to ill-health, and lack of awareness as to the handling techniques required for the more dangerous substances all require to be looked at, and nothing left to chance.

1. Management

The following areas will need to be analysed in order to ascertain the training needs of the management group. Therefore, knowledge is required of the following:

(a) the organisational policy on health and safety; knowledge of the policy – if any exists; knowledge of the need for a policy if one does not exist;
(b) the areas of highest cost with regard to accidents or industrial disease, strain and stress;
(c) management; the ultimate responsibility for safety;
(d) responsibility for safety that should be carried by local and line managers and supervisors;
(e) employers' and owner occupiers' responsibility for safety;
(f) factory and other statutory law; the common law relative to the industrial accident and the injury at work; the employer's liability;
(g) the investigation of accidents and incidents; action on the causes;
(h) premises inspections (including all the facilities);
(i) safety hazards (spilt liquids on access areas, ineffective guards);
(j) the standard documented safety system in use – the *safety policy*;
(k) the attitudes towards training of staff;
(l) mandatory requirement with regard to protective clothing for the particular process and the working environment.

The promotion of safety. The joint consultation with the safety manager, the staff and the employer or head of the business. A simplistic approach and a convincing argument as to the value of health and safety at work for all in the business.

THE INITIATIVE HAS TO BE TAKEN BY THE EMPLOYER, OR THE DESIGNATED HEAD OF THE BUSINESS.

2. Supervision
It is imperative that any person who is delegated authority within any area of the organisation is fully aware of the implications of the Health and Safety at Work Act 1974, and all the accompanying Codes of Practice and the attendant Regulations, the industrial and commercial application of the law and the philosophy in real terms, and not a matter of 'lip service'.

(a) The organisational policy. Knowledge of the policy of the business.

ALL EMPLOYERS ARE OBLIGED TO HAVE A SAFETY POLICY STRUCTURED TO THEIR PARTICULAR ORGANISATION AND PROPERLY DISPLAYED.

(b) to support the management's responsibility towards safety;
(c) to monitor the employees responsibility towards safety – Section 7 of the Health and Safety at Work Act 1974;
(d) factory and common law – the employer's liability;
(e) investigation of accidents; the instant and accurate reporting of!;
(f) periodic inspection of the premises under the immediate control of the supervisor in question; hazard spotting;
(g) accident prevention, both the theoretical and the practical approach;
(h) joint consultation; the management and the employees at all levels;
(i) loss control techniques; the spotting of absence through ill-health;
(j) induction training – new employees to be thoroughly versed in the employer's policy and the expectations of performance;
(k) first aid requirements and the provisions for emergency treatment;
(l) safety hazards, e.g. housekeeping, safe access and egress to premises;
(m) FIRE PREVENTION: fire drills, fire fighting – minimal requirements; the appropriate fire extinguisher for the particular fire.

It has to be said that many foremen and supervisors have, in the past, placed the above at the bottom of their lists of duties and performance, sometimes due to the general laxity within the particular business and sometimes through a lack of awareness of interest on their part.

3. Employees and young persons
No matter the possible reluctance to either 'get involved' or to 'be bothered' with such matters as health and safety, SOMETIMES THE

PHILOSOPHY AND THE ATTITUDE OF THE ORDINARY WORKER AND YOUNG PERSON LEAVES A LOT TO BE DESIRED WHEN MATTERS OF SERIOUSNESS OR IMPORT ARE PUT TO THEM 'IT WILL NOT HAPPEN TO ME!'

The employer should make it a condition of employment that all staff are required to take note of these matters. Indeed, it is a matter of legal responsibility on the part of the employee that he or she take note of the appropriate Section (7) of the Health and Safety at Work Act 1974, and the Safety Policy of the employer, which the employer is also required to implement and display. Should any member of the work-force disregard these matters, then the option of dismissal is open to the employer – provided that the employer operates a reasonable procedure related to discipline.

THE FOLLOWING SHOULD BE BROUGHT TO THE ATTEN-TION OF THE EMPLOYEE:

(a) the Company Safety Policy; knowledge of the policy;
(b) the management's responsibilities; the procedure for communication;
(c) the employee's responsibilities.

Factory law indicates these responsibilities well enough and this Brief is designed to 'put into the mind' of all within an organisation an awareness of the overall responsibility for the health, safety and welfare provisions:

(d) knowledge of the factory law, a basic awareness;
(e) induction training – job instruction with emphasis on safety;
(f) good housekeeping – the cleanliness of the workplace;
(g) the matter of 'horse-play' or 'skylarking' at work; the disciplinary consequences of such misconduct – Section 7 of the Health and Safety at Work Act 1974;
(h) fire drill; first aid; basic knowledge of the company fire policy;
(i) protective clothing – the requirement to wear in the danger areas of the workplace; the remedy if ignored;
(j) manual handling – techniques to avoid injury;
(k) personal hygiene; general housekeeping within the workplace;
(l) the training in the use of chemicals within the workplace; the requirement to observe the Company Storage Policy on the proper and safe areas to hold stocks of chemicals, and the disciplinary rules of the company that relate to mis-use, or alleged ignorance of the company's chemical usage and storage policy.
(m) the duty of the employee to observe any particular policy on smoking that might be in force.

4. General points to note

To sum up the matters in this section it is now obvious to the employer that the prime concern for all in any particular business is the health, safety and welfare of the workforce. It is a sad fact of life that health and safety at work is often the least of the average employer's worries. The running of the business is, of itself, often enough to occupy the full attention of any employer. However, the fact of the matter is that the Statutory law, the Common law and the various Regulations, Codes of Practice and, indeed, the possible future success of the business can depend upon the general awareness as explained above. So take the trouble to note this Brief and implement its philosophy.

Thoughts on the implementation of safety policies

In the United Kingdom there are over 90,000,000 periods of incapacity when employees are aware from work through an accident or an incident leading to stress, strain or injury per year. There are 30,000,000 minor injuries and more than 150,000,000 property damage incidents. This situation will continue just as long as management, employees and safety staff allow the luxury of negative thinking rather than concentrating their minds. The damage to the small business can be crippling if, for example, a fire was caused through careless attention to detail – cigarette end smouldering in a flammable area. Faulty electrical appliances and wiring.

Here are some examples of the negative thinking that contributes to problems:

1. *I have done this for years, I will not CHANGE!*
2. *We have tried it before, it will not work.*
3. *Our business is different* (it can still burn down)
4. *Its a good idea but the timing is bad, we cannot really implement measures.*
5. *Lets think about it and try it in a month's time.*
6. *Too much paper work, lets go on as we are.*
7. *Too costly, we cannot afford it.* If the business is viable?
8. *Our policy will not permit a change.*
9. *Its all too complicated, our workpeople cannot or will not understand!*
10. *What was good enough in the old days is OK for the future as well.*

Tradition has a great deal to do with this in that people are reluctant to adopt new ideas or working practices, that the accepted way to manage is the right way and that to concentrate too much on the health, safety and welfare of the employee might smell of paternalism. This is a false notion. The whole area of the business enterprise must improve by adopting the proper approach to good housekeeping, health, safety and welfare.

The Health and Safety at Work Act 1974 explained

The following is an in-depth examination of the Act, its meaning and aims.

The 1974 Act is an 'enabling' device, and a general rather than a detailed piece of legislation designed to cover all in employment, including those in the transport, postal, entertainment, medical services and education, all areas that were formerly unprotected by the previously fragmented legislation that covered safety at work. It does not stipulate precise and specific legal requirements in the field of health and safety, as does, for example, the Factory Act of 1961, but instead imposes general duties on employers and on workers, in the hope of achieving the following stated aims and being overtly and deliberately broad in the terms of safety reference:

(a) securing the health, safety and welfare of persons at work;
(b) protecting others from the hazards arising from work activities;
(c) regulating the acquisition, storage and use of all dangerous substances;
(d) controlling air pollution;
(e) controlling the use and storage of chemicals in the workplace.

The most important part of the Act is the first of the five purposes as listed above, and holds the greatest importance for the employer and the employee. The general duties as expressed under the Act should be the goal of all in work.

The statutory duties: Section 2

The general duties imposed by the Act are, by and large, those which, under the common law give rise to claims for damages in the civil courts then they are neglected. Their statutory requirements as restated here, however, make culpable breach of them a criminal offence also – against which factory inspectors and other enforcement officers may institute legal proceedings. Legal proceedings can only be avoided by the employer taking the basic precautions in the running of the business. Prosecutions can prove costly for the employer, with fines and even, in extreme cases, prison sentences being imposed for particular and blatant disregard for the basic safety of the employee or third parties that have been affected by the employer's operation.

General duties

Section 2: general duties of employers to their employees

1. It shall be the duty of every employer to ensure, so far as is reasonably practicable, the health, safety and welfare at work of all his employees.
2. Without prejudice to the generality of an employer's duty under the preceding sub-section, the matters to which that duty extends include in particular:
   (a) the provision and maintenance of plant and systems of work that are, so far as is reasonably practicable, safe and without risks to health;
   (b) arrangements for ensuring, so far as is reasonably practicable, the safety and absence of risks to health in connection with the use, handling, storage and transport of articles and substances;
   (c) the provision of such information, instruction, training and supervision as is necessary to ensure, as far as is reasonably practicable, the health and safety at work of his or her employees;
   (d) so far as is reasonably practicable as regards any place of work under the employer's control, the maintenance of it in a condition that is without risks and safe, and the provision and maintenance of means of access to and egress from it that are safe and without risks;
   (e) the provision and maintenance of a working environment for his or her employees that is, so far as is reasonably practicable, safe, without risks to health, and adequate as regards facilities and arrangements for their welfare at work.
3. Except in cases as may be prescribed, it shall be the duty of every employer to prepare and as often as may be to revise a WRITTEN STATEMENT OF HIS OR HER GENERAL POLICY WITH RESPECT TO THE HEALTH AND SAFETY AT WORK OF HIS/HER EMPLOYEES and the organisation and arrangements for the time being in force for carrying out of that policy, and to bring this statement and any revision of it to the notice of all his or her employees.

Section 3: general duties of employers and self-employed to persons other than their employees

1. It shall be the duty of every employer to conduct his or her undertaking in such a way as to ensure, so far as is reasonably practicable, that persons not in his/her employment who may be affected thereby are not thereby exposed to risks to their health or safety.

2. It shall be the duty of every self-employed person to conduct his or her undertaking in such a way as to ensure, so far as is reasonably practicable, that he/she and the other persons (not being his/her employees) who may be affected thereby are not thereby exposed to risks to their health and safety.

3. In such cases as may be prescribed, it shall be the duty of every employer and self-employed person, in the prescribed manner and in the prescribed circumstances, to give to persons (not being his or her employees) who may be affected by the way in which he/she conducts his/her undertaking the prescribed information about such aspects of the way in which he/she conducts his/her undertaking as might affect their health and safety.

THE ABOVE IS OF IMMEDIATE RELEVANCE AND IMPORT-
ANCE TO YOUR COMPANY, THERE ARE MANY OTHER
SECTIONS WITHIN THE ACT WHICH CAN BE EXPLAINED
AS AND WHEN REQUESTED. SECTION 7 – WHICH FOLLOWS
– IS OF DIRECT RELEVANCE AND IMPORTANCE TO YOUR
EMPLOYEES, WHO SHOULD ALL BE MADE AWARE OF THE
CONTENT AND IMPORT OF THE SECTION.

Section 7: general duties of employees at work
It shall be the duty of every employee while at work:

(a) to take reasonable care for the health and safety of himself or herself and of other persons who may be affected by his/her acts or his/her omissions at work; and

(b) as regards any duty or requirement imposed on his or her employer or any other person by or under any of the relevant statutory provisions, to co-operate with him/her so far as is reasonably practicable and necessary to enable that duty or requirement to be performed or complied with.

Section 8: duty not to interfere with or misuse things provided pursuant to certain provisions for health and safety
No person shall intentionally or recklessly interfere with or misuse

anything provided in the interests of health, safety or welfare in pursuance of any of the statutory provisions.

THE ABOVE SECTIONS ARE STATUTORY PROVISIONS. THEREFORE, SHOULD ANY EMPLOYEE KNOWINGLY BREACH THE EMPLOYER'S RULES THAT HAVE BEEN SET DOWN TO CONFORM WITH THE ABOVE SECTIONS, THEN THAT EMPLOYEE WILL HAVE COMMITTED AN ACT OF *GROSS MISCONDUCT*. THE REMEDY FOR THAT MIGHT WELL BE DISMISSAL.

NOTE: It is well established by case precedent as recorded in the Industrial Tribunal Law Reports, that employees who have been dismissed for a breach of the employer's rules relative to health and safety at work, have been dismissed FAIRLY. It is important that a proper disciplinary procedure is followed, even in extreme cases of breach. The reader should further note that some employees have been subject to criminal prosecution brought by the Health and Safety Executive.

Check-lists

In this part of the Brief I have laid out certain check-lists that will indicate the employer's willingness to both co-operate with, and enter into, the spirit of the health and safety philosophy of both the Health and Safety Commission and the Health and Safety Executive, thus tempering any unexpected visit by an enforcing official, in that the official will read from the Safety Manual the employer's INTENT, and, therefore, this will probably lead to an advisory report and a critique of any unsafe practice that might be noted during the inspection he or she has carried out, rather than a censorious report that could lead to a prosecution – should an inadvertent breach of the Statute be discovered.

Welfare
Has the place of work:

(a) an adequate supply of wholesome drinking water?
(b) satisfactory washing facilities (hot and cold water, soap, clean linen, adequate number of wash basins, showers were necessary)?
(c) suitable toilet accommodation (enough in number, screened for privacy; fitted with locks; kept clean; provided separately for men and women)?

(d) satisfactory storage space for clothes not worn during working hours (clean lockers or clothes pegs for each individual worker in a ventilated and adequately guarded area, and adequate drying areas and facilities for wet clothing to be properly aired and dried)?

(e) an adequate number of sufficiently well-designed seats for those whose tasks can be carried out while they are seated?

(f) has the workplace a notice board for the display of the works rules relative to the storage and use of any chemicals on site?

(g) regularly maintained and easily accessible first-aid boxes or cupboards; persons trained and regularly given refresher courses in first-aid; fool-proof plans to summon medical aid in the event of an accident or a sudden illness?

Working conditions

Is the place of work:

(a) kept clean (cleared of dirt and refuse; floors cleaned regularly; walls and ceilings washed and redecorated as necessary)? NOTE: some particular Regulations demand that the washing shall be within certain periods of time.

(b) spacious enough to work in or is the workplace overcrowded? (is there 400 cubic feet of space for each worker?)

(c) sufficiently ventilated, especially if there are dust and fumes about (smoking by employees, dusty processes?)

(d) of a reasonable temperature, and is there a thermometer available to measure the temperature of the actual working area?

(e) well or badly lit? and has the lighting been examined recently?

NOTE: MUCH OF THE ABOVE IS NOT RELEVANT TO THE WELL-RUN BUSINESS, BUT THE LIST IS ENDLESS AND IS ADAPTABLE TO THE PARTICULAR WORKPLACE AND THE ENVIRONMENT. NOTHING IS PERFECT AND THERE IS ALWAYS ROOM FOR IMPROVEMENT.

CHECK-LISTS FOR CLIENTS WITH SPECIALISED WORKPLACES CAN BE PREPARED AS AND WHEN REQUIRED.

Fire precautions

(a) Is the workplace fire certificate up-to-date – has the number of workers increased, or the amount of inflammable material stored on the premises increased. Has the building had structure changes since the last inspection?

(b) Are all fire-exits properly maintained, clearly indicated, and kept UNOBSTRUCTED?

(c) Are fire-resistant doors kept closed?

(d) Does the employer organise regular FIRE DRILLS and train the employees in the evacuation of the premises in the event of an emergency? Do the employees know the means of EXIT in the event of a fire or any other emergency?

(e) Is the fire alarm – if fitted – clearly audible from all areas of the workplace, and tested at least every three months?

(f) Is the fire-fighting equipment easily accessible, well maintained, properly suitable for the particular hazard that might arise, e.g. an electrical fault leading to a fire and the type of extinguish that is designed for that type of fire?

(g) Is anyone within the workforce trained in the use of the fire-fighting equipment?

(h) Are all highly inflammable materials at the workplace clearly and accurately labelled; kept to a minimum; stored as far as possible away from the working areas – paints, chemicals or flammable cleaning fluids stored near any workplace heating equipment such as electric fires or calor gas fires?

(i) ash trays cleared after use; cigarette ends – still alight – put into waste bags; faulty electric plugs; plugs left alive after working hours or in their sockets after use?

NOTE: ALL MATTERS RELATING TO FIRE HAZARD CAN BE DEALT WITH BY THE FIRE PREVENTION OFFICER WHO CAN BE CONTACTED AT THE LOCAL FIRE STATION.

Safety policies

The law is quite specific as to safety policies. The law states that it has to be the employer's responsibility and his or her duty to formulate a safety policy. The Health and Safety at Work Act 1974 requires that every employer must produce a safety policy, make it known to his/her employees, and to bring it up to date when necessary.

THE FOLLOWING IS THE CORRECT APPROACH:

1. A written statement of his or her general policy with respect to the health and safety at work of his employees, and the organisation and the arrangements for the time being in force for the carrying out of that policy.

2. Such a policy statement has a great potential as a base for a thorough-going campaign to achieve a safe and healthy workplace,

and often will – if it is positive and comprehensive enough – be a good indication of the degree of an employer's intent and his or her own commitment to radical remedial action and consultation.

3. Although the omission from the Act of any real definition or indeed qualification of this statement – a suggestion of what would go to constitute a 'reasonable statement', for instance, – weakens its legal status, the Health and Safety Commission has issued certain guidance notes on what it expects an employer's Safety Policy to contain, and these can be considered by the employer when the policy is being prepared.

The statement of intent: the basic elements of a 'good' safety policy

(a) the employer's own commitment;
(b) a definition of who is responsible for what aspects of health and safety throughout the undertaking;
(c) the identification of hazards to be avoided, the precautions to be taken and the procedures to be observed;
(d) the proper display of the works rules and regulations and the Statute Rules and Regulations for safety at work.

NOTE: It is good practice to write into the contract of employment a clause stipulating that the employee must obey the rules relative to health and safety at work, with the possible penalty for infringement made clear.

The main ingredients of the statement of intent

(a) an intention to treat the basic legal requirements as minimum rather than as maximum; motivated by commitment and not a mere reiteration of the employer's legal obligations;
(b) a promise that concern for health and safety will be as great as concern over matters of production, customer service, finance and the viability of the company;
(c) a commitment to provide adequate funds and details of how money will be spent or made available to be utilised for the promotion of safety;
(d) a declaration that the workplace health and safety will always be taken into account where any new policies that may have a bearing on it are decided (when new products, processes, premises are being considered, for example);
(e) an affirmation that management alone is responsible for providing a safe and healthy working environment;
(f) a commitment to genuine consultations over matters of health and

safety and welfare, both with outside agencies and internally –
from all employed in the organisation;

(g) the details of training for and disclosure of information to all the
employees in the area of health and safety on the job.

Definition of managerial responsibilities

These will vary from workplace to workplace, but should certainly lay
down that the overall responsibility for health and safety rests at the
highest level with a named executive – the senior manager or the owner
of the business, and that access to him or her will have priority in all
the related matters of health and safety at work.

A definite division of responsibilities is to be organised for making
the policy work in specified departments, work areas, etc., and for
establishing agreed procedures between named individuals at middle-
management.

By stipulating exactly where responsibility lies in the above terms,
and by also ensuring that responsibility rests in each case with an
APPROPRIATE INDIVIDUAL, the employer can greatly ease the
burden on himself or herself, always remembering that, at the end of
the day, he/she alone is the ultimate for total responsibility within his
organisation.

The identification of hazards, precautions, procedures, etc., largely
speaks for itself. In certain undertakings where the work is – in the
main – complex, it will, of course, prove impossible to deal compre-
hensively in the policy statement with the potential hazards, but,
clearly, the main statement must make reference to them and to the
particular working manuals or professional standards that particular
tasks require, accessible to the employees where more detailed information is required and readily available.

This section should make particular reference to:

(a) any dangerous machinery, equipment, processes, etc.;
(b) any toxic substances in use or likely to be created due to work
processes;
(c) the specific legal regulations that have a bearing on these hazards;
(d) the precautions to be taken at all times where particular hazards
might arise, including food storage, food handling in catering
establishments, chemicals and flammable liquids where these materials are part of the everyday process;
(e) FIRST AID arrangements;
(g) FIRE DRILLS and procedures in the event of a fire or an
emergency;
(h) where appropriate, a 'PERMIT TO WORK' safeguard instituted
when plant and machinery is being serviced.

The notification of accidents and dangerous occurrences: The Regulations – as at 1986 – and current

It is required by Statute – enacted in 1980 and valid law in 1981 – that all accidents and dangerous occurrences arising at work and through the work processes must be recorded, and in certain noted circumstances reported to the Health and Safety Executive depending upon the severity of the event. The classic types of the reportable accident and hazardous occurrence are quoted in this part of the Brief and must be carefully noted.

Definition of 'notifiable' accident and dangerous occurrence

Notifiable accident

Accidents at work will require to be notified to the Executive if they arise out of, or in connection with work, and either of the following criteria apply:

(a) results in the death of, or the major injury to any person; or
(b) in the case of an employee at work, results in that employee being incapacitated for work for more than three consecutive days – excluding the day of the accident and any Sunday, or if Sunday is not a rest day, then one rest day.

MAJOR INJURY means:

(a) fracture of the skull, spine or pelvis;
(b) fracture of any bone:
   (i) in the arm, other than a bone in the wrist or hand,
   (ii) in the leg, other than a bone in the ankle or foot,
(c) amputation of a hand or foot;
(d) the loss of the sight of an eye;
(e) any other injury which results in the person injured being admitted to hospital as an in-patient for more than twenty-four hours, unless that person is detained for observation only.

Notifiable dangerous occurrences

Dangerous occurrences at the workplace that require to be notified to the Health and Safety Executive are as follows:

1. The collapse or overturning of any lift, hoist, or crane, excavation or mobile powered access platform, or failure of any load-bearing part of the above, which, taking into account the circumstances of the occurrences might have been liable to cause a MAJOR

INJURY to any person – either an employee of the company or third parties.

2. Explosion, collapse or bursting of any closed vessel including a boiler or boiler tube in which there was any gas – including air – or vapour at a pressure greater than atmospheric which might have been liable to cause MAJOR INJURY to any person – either an employee or third parties – or which resulted in significant damage to the plant or the premises.

3. Electrical short circuit or overload attended by a fire or by an explosion which resulted in the stoppage of the plant involved for more than twenty-four hours and which, taking into account the circumstances of the occurrence, might have been liable to cause MAJOR INJURY to any person – employee of the company or third parties.

4. An explosion or fire occurring at any plant or place which has resulted in the stoppage of the plant or suspension of normal work in that place for more than twenty-four hours, where such explosion or fire was due to the ignition of process materials, their by-products (including waste) or finished products.

5. The sudden, uncontrolled release of one tonne or more of highly flammable liquid, flammable gas or flammable liquid above its boiling point from any system or plant or pipe-line.

6. A collapse or part collapse of any scaffold which is more than twelve metres high which results in a substantial part of the scaffold falling or overturning.

7. The uncontrolled release or escape of any substances or agents in circumstances which, having regard to the nature of the substance or agent and the extent and location of the release or escape, might be liable to cause damage to the health of – or MAJOR INJURY to – any person.

8. Any incident in which any person is affected by the inhalation, ingestion or other absorption of any substance, or by the lack of oxygen, to such an extent as to cause acute ill-health requiring medical treatment.

9. Any case of acute ill-health where there is reason to believe that this resulted from occupational exposure to isolated pathogens or infected material.

10. Any ignition or explosion of explosives, where the ignition or explosion was not intentional.

The employer's records

Particulars to be kept in records of accidents and dangerous occurrences are as follows:

(a) In the case of either, the date, location and the time as near as is reasonably practicable, and a brief description of the circumstances.

(b) In the case of an accident, the following particulars of the person injured: name; sex; occupation; age; nature of the injury; where the accident occurred.

(c) In the case of ill-health, record as above with the addition of the nature of the disease for which the claim was made, and the date of the first absence from work. IMPORTANT AS A MATTER OF RECORD IN THE EVENT OF A CLAIM AGAINST THE EMPLOYER.

Notification procedure

Where there is a notifiable accident resulting from work and ending in the death of – or MAJOR INJURY to – any person, or there is a notifiable dangerous occurrence, the responsible person – the employer; owner; the delegated management shall:

(a) forthwith notify the enforcing authority – the Health and Safety Executive – and by the quickest practicable means; and

(b) within seven days send a report of the incident to the enforcing authority on a form approved by the authority for the purpose of the Regulations by the Health and Safety Executive.

Duty to notify the death of an employee

Subject to the Regulations, where an employee has suffered an injury as a result of a notifiable accident or notifiable dangerous occurrence which is the cause or a cause of his or her death within one year of the date of the accident or dangerous occurrence, the employer shall inform the enforcing authority – the Health and Safety Executive – in writing of the death as soon as it comes to his or her knowledge, whether or not the accident had been notified under the Regulations at the time of the event.

Duty of the employer to make provision for first-aid

1. An employer shall provide, or ensure that there are provided, such facilities and equipment as are adequate and appropriate in the circumstances for enabling first-aid to be rendered to his or her employees if they are injured or become ill at work.

2. An employer shall provide, or ensure that there is provided, such a

number of suitable persons as adequate in the circumstances for the rendering of first-aid to his or her employees if they become ill or are injured whilst at work – dependent upon the size of the business.

Summary

All employers, regardless of the size of their business, should ensure that their priorities include much of what is in this Brief. At first sight, there appears to be a massive amount of regulation and restriction on the running of the day-to-day operations of any business and to a certain extent that might well be the case. However, it must be obvious to any employer that the business profitability depends upon a fit and present workforce, whether or not there are many or few employed. The major asset to any employer has to be his or her labour force and that his/her labour force is present when the business requires it.

The Health and Safety at Work Act 1974 goes a long way to ensuring that the majority of employees have a reasonably practicable level of safety and healthy conditions at work. It is really down to the employer to follow the reasoning as laid out in this Brief, and so ensure the health and safety and, not to be forgotten, welfare, of his or her workforce.

Last but not least, the employees in any organisation must have the basic training in the matter of FIRE PRECAUTIONS, FIRST AID, the whereabouts of FIRST-AID BOXES, the standard of behaviour expected of them in matters of safety, and the obedience of the workforce to all rules and regulations applicable to these matters. It is, of course, a matter of the greatest importance that the employer has a full and proper procedure of discipline and grievances, so that the employees are in no doubt as to their own responsibilities at work. Too often it is said by those who have breached the rules of a workplace, that THEY DID NOT KNOW THAT THAT ACTION WAS WRONG. Dismissal might then be technically unfair, if that is the option that the employer chooses.

Index